fish & brewis
toutens & tales

Recipes and Recollections
from St. Leonard's, Newfoundland

fish & brewis toutens & tales

Recipes and Recollections from St. Leonard's, Newfoundland

Len Margaret

BREAKWATER
Canada's Atlantic Publisher

Illustration credits:

Salt fish, Rounder, Mussels, Turnip, Cabbage, Bread, Pastry, Liza's Rock — **Gerry Squires**

St. Leonard's map graphics — **Warrick Hewitt**

All other drawings — **Amie Albert**

Photographs pages viii ix 30 31 34 37 — **Eugene Follett**

Printed in Canada

CANADA'S ATLANTIC FOLKLORE AND FOLKLIFE SERIES NO. 7, 1980
Consulting Editor, Kenneth S. Goldstein

Canadian Cataloguing in Publication Data

Margaret, Len.
  Fish & brewis, toutens & tales

(Canada's Atlantic folklore and folklife series; 7
ISSN 0708-4226)

ISBN 0-919948-36-7 paper
ISBN 0-919948-37-5 cloth

1. Folk-lore — Newfoundland — St. Leonard's.
2. Cookery, Canadian — Newfoundland.* I. Title.
II. Series.

GR113.M37   398.2'09718   C79-094633-5

To Oliver Leonard
and those who came after

NEWFOUNDLAND

St. Leonard's

Placentia Bay

Indeed, yes, what feeds we used to have. Lovely stuff that we were reared on and now get only as a special treat for there never seems to be enough roasted partridge and fried trout to go around.

Here are the genuine recipes from St. Leonard's on the western side of "That Far Greater Bay"...but, more than that, there are glimpses of the background against which all this dreadful good grub was consumed.

This book should do much to balance the picture too many people have of outport life, grim, glum images of storms, shipwrecks, semi-starvation and busted appendixes.

Fish & Brewis, Toutens & Tales tells us about bright lamps, warm kitchens and full and contented people. It proves that we not only endured but we also enjoyed.

Ray Guy

The original name of St. Leonard's was Oliver's Cove. Oliver Leonard, born in England 1740, married Sophia Langford in 1760. Edward, son of Oliver and Sophia, married Olive Abbott in 1776, at Oliver's Cove.

Two of the five abandoned houses remaining in St. Leonard's (May 1978)

Ned Leonard's house in ruins and The Head behind (May 1978)

Jim Leonard's house in ruins (May 1978)

The Ghost Ship

It was a still night in August. I waited fearfully, although my uncle was with me, hoping to see the ghost ship that appeared in the Reach always about this time of year.

It was a bit scary, sitting there, in the pitch black dark with my knees hunched under my chin and my back pressed against the breakwater. I almost wished I hadn't come, but I had begged my uncle to take me here ever since Billy and his father had climbed Calvary Hill to watch the sun dance on Easter morning. I wasn't feeling a bit brave like Billy said he was. I wished I was up in the house, looking through the window at the Reach instead of here under the breakwater. Every little sound made me nervous and when a stone rolled from the cliffside, I waited for it to drop in the landwash, but it didn't. I wondered about that.

The sea was calm except for the small lops that sighed and gurgled around the kelpy rocks on the beach and I never thought a night could be so dark. I couldn't see my uncle's face but I was able to make out the glow of the ashes on his pipe and the smell of the tobacco drifted across my face. I coughed and the sound echoed in the cliffs of the Cove. A dog barked far back in a yard and it sounded like a whole pack as the echoes bounced back from the hill. Someone slammed a door and the night was still again.

My uncle shifted his weight. "We'll soon see her now," he said and went on to tell of the times he had watched her from the jiggin' cove as if it was just the *Home* or the *Argyle* we had come here to see.

"There's her top lights now," he said. "See how she sits in the water? When she comes handier up the Reach, you'll be able to see her lower deck all lit up. She's a steamer of some kind with her flag at half-mast and there's never any smoke comin' from her funnels." He scratched a match on the tap of his boot and relit his pipe.

"Can you hear the music now?" he asked me.

The wind was beginning to rise. It swished in the crags on the hillside and made the stage door squeak on its hinges. Sea-fires glinted on the mooring ropes as the motor-boats swayed on the collar.

"She looks good, all lit up like that," I said because I didn't want to disappoint him. "Maybe grown-up people are the only ones allowed to see ghost ships," I said to myself without speaking, but I'd still be able to describe her to Billy, word for word, just like my uncle had described her to me.

After a while, he tapped the tobacco from his pipe and stood up. "I have to copper my punt tomorrow," he said, "that's if it don't rain or something."

A clear spot lumed in the sky over the Red Land and the waves splashed high in the landwash.

I kept close to him as we walked up the lane and hoped for his sake he really believed that I had seen the ghost ship.

I told Billy all about her one evening just before dark, when we were sitting on the breakwater with nothing better to do.

Feastdays and Rites

St. Bridget

St. Bridget's feastday was February 1st. "Feast Day" was an expression used in relation to the calendar of the saints. The people of Irish descent regarded St. Bridget, who was noted for her works of charity among the poor, as the second patron saint of Ireland. She founded a monastry at Kildare and was nicknamed "Mary of the Gael." On St. Bridget's night, little bags were hung on the fence to receive her blessings and little crosses were wittled to place over the door. These were called St. Bridget's cross.

*   *   *

Candlemas

Candlemas Day was celebrated on February 2nd. At Mass that day candles were blessed and distributed among the parishioners. The candles were lit and three drops of the melted wax dropped in caps and hats as a religious gesture in honour of the day.

The older folks predicted the forecast of winters by the weather on Candlemas day.

"If Candlemas day comes in clear and fine,
    The worst of the winter is left behind."

"If Candlemas day comes in foul and glum,
    The worst of the winter is yet to come."

"If the crows fly low,
    We'll have plenty of snow."

*   *   *

St. Blaise

St. Blaise was honoured by attending evening devotions and the Blessing of Throats. This ceremony was administered by the priest in honour of St. Blaise who, it was said, saved the life of a boy who had swallowed a fishbone. The blessing was given in the hope of preventing throat infection. The feastday was February 3rd.

* * *

Shrove Tuesday

The day before Ash Wednesday was reserved strictly for special dinners and family entertainment in anticipation of the fast and abstinence of the Lenten season. Dancing, cardplaying, weddings and public social gatherings were prohibited during the forty days of Lent.

The vegetables were taken from the cellar the previous evening and shared with neighbours who may not have had enough of the varieties to last up to this time of the year.

The puddings were mixed and put in separate pudding bags ahead of time. The meat (rabbit, venison, fresh beef or seabirds) was selected and made ready.

Breakfast consisted of oatmeal porridge, hot buttered toast and tea. There would be no strenuous labours executed this particular day. Only the milking and attending to the needs of the livestock, stacking firewood and making enough splits to carry over until Thursday. There would be no axe used on Ash Wednesday.

Dinner would be a generous meal of meats with rich brown gravy, figgy duff, bread puddings, peas pudding, cabbage, potatoes, turnip, carrots and salt beef. Sauce was always made to be served with left-over raisin or boiled bread pudding.

When the table was set, the family sat and grace was recited by the oldest member. Before eating, however, a little ceremony was performed. This ritual was firmly believed to ensure a bountiful harvest and good luck in all family endeavours until the next Shrove Tuesday when the ceremony would be repeated.

A small toggle was carved from a piece of birch or other hardwood earlier in the day. Then a small piece of the puddings made from flour, a piece of salt meat and a cube of bread would be pushed on to the toggle and hung over the outside door-facing. This being accomplished with all due respect, the family were allowed to begin eating.

After dinner the father and older members of the family sat back and chatted at will while the mother and female members cleaned the dishes and put the kitchen to rights.

Pancakes were always the supper dish for Shrove Tuesday. Although every pancake was consumed, the meal was more of a lark for the youngsters. The recipe was no different from any pancake mixture except the addition of symbols that were thrown into it. It was a type of fortune telling to tell what you'd be when you grew up, and each contribution had its own particular meaning. A portion of the batter was used for this and only one item was put into each pancake so that none of the children could get more than his share of fortune telling. The meaning of each item was as follows:

ring— husband or wife
straw — farmer
match — boatbuilder
nail — carpenter
button — bachelor or old maid
medal — a priest or nun
money — rich man or woman
linen — tailor or seamstress

It sounds like a hazard to have such things hidden in your supper, but as far as I can recall no one in St. Leonard's ever choked on a nail or swallowed a ring.

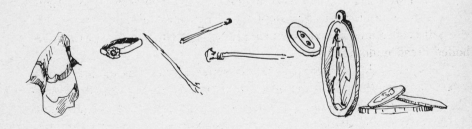

St. Patrick

St. Patrick's Day on March 17th was a holy day and a holiday. It was celebrated with religious ceremonies, the wearing of shamrocks, green ribbons, green ties for the men and green blouses or dresses for the women. The day was set apart from Lenten fast so that an Irish concert could be put off in the parish hall at night. The concert was followed by a dance and the music of the fiddle, accordion, tin whistle or mouth organ could be heard until the stroke of twelve. Then it was back to fasting for the rest of Lent.

* * *

Mid Summer

Mid Summer's Day was the 24th of June. The young people indulged in all kinds of rituals that were supposed to predict their future. They didn't always believe in these rites but had a lot of fun doing them.

(1) Break an egg, separate the yolk from the white. Place the white in half a glass of cold water and put it in the window before the sun rises. When the sun shines on the glass containing the egg-white, the heat of the sun will cause the egg-white to rise in fantastic shapes of rigged ships, castles and towers or any object your imagination can conjure up. If the contents didn't rise at all, then you will have bad luck.

(2) If you wanted to tempt fate and risk the consequences, you had the option of throwing the egg that didn't rise on the garden path. The first man to walk over it would bear the initials of your lover.

(3) Rise before sun-up. Take two garden snails and put them between two smoked plates and set them in a level spot in the garden. Remove the top plate at noon and you will find the initials of your future husband traced on the other plate.

* * *

St. Swithen

St. Swithin's Day, July 15th, predicted the weather for forty days after the feastday. St. Swithin was the English bishop of Winchester and when he was dying, requested that his body be interred outside his church. A new church was built in his honour many years later and his remains were transferred to the new burial ground. If it rains on St. Swithin's Day, there will be rainy weather for forty consecutive days after.

* * *

Lady Day

August 15th was Lady Day. The parish which consisted of about twelve settlements, was named in honour of the Assumption of Our Lady. The celebration and religious rites date as far back as 1850, when Father James Walsh was appointed parish priest of St. Kyrans.

The Garden Party was the prime event. People came from the harbours, coves and islands to take part in the celebrations. They came in sail boats, trap skiffs and dories. It was a special day, a day of feasting, dancing, games and fun. But the most important thing was the opportunity to meet friends and relations and to be sociable. This was one day the conversation was casual and relaxed. There would be no mention of the loss of fishing gear or the menace of dogfish, the lack of bait or the price of the summer's catch, and everyone welcomed the opportunity to divest themselves of all domestic concern.

There were card games, raffles, tug-o-war, and target shooting, and there were guessing games, grab bags and sack races for the children. The women served teas and dinners all through the day. Tables were set up in the hall where the women proudly displayed their donations of baked goods.

Long tables covered with fancy cloths and vases of fresh flowers were reserved for those who wished to dine. There were dishes of cold meats, tureens of hot meat and gravy, varieties of home-made bread and fancy biscuits. Cakes came as a special donation from each settlement and were swathed in foamy white frosting, decorated with 'tens-of-thousands' and 'silver shot' and displayed on cut glass plates. They were not served as a rule, but were auctioned off to the highest bidder before the dining area was closed.

When evening came, the tables were dismantled and the floor cleared for dancing. Step dancing and waltzing were competitive dances but everyone engaged in the Square Dance, Virginia Reel and the Lancers.

Garden parties were something to look forward to all year long.

Pastimes

When the weather got warm and most of the moisture left by melting snow and spring rains had dried up in the lanes and on the road, we started rolling hoops. The hoops were made of tin. They were left over from discarded flour barrels. It was important that the hoop be perfectly round. The slightest bend in the circumference made it difficult to control a hoop going down grade or around fence corners.

We painted our sticks and tacked short coloured streamers on one end and after practicing around the lanes for a week or so, we began racing from the Cove to the Old Church and back.

We sang as we rolled our hoops. Some of our favourites were verses from such songs as Darling Nellie Grey and My Old Kentucky Home. Sometimes, we made up our own.

Our hoops are rolling swiftly on
Past hill and dale and Chapel Pond.
Around the bend to Mrs. Dunn's and
back again.
We race the clouds, the wind, the rain
and roll them down the grassy lane to
home once more.

In the Spring of the year, when the last bally-carter had slipped into the water and the beach was all patches of fine clean sand, we ran to search for curiosities.

We gathered everything in sight, dead star fish, gulls' feathers, hoars eggs, chains, driftwood, and stones tumbled smooth and gleaming by the constant motion of the undertow.

North-east winds threw up a fair amount of glass floats and tolepins and if we were lucky we might find the skeleton of a seabird. We brought our treasures home, but always with strict instructions that they were to be left in the yard at our own risk.

* * *

Hide and Seek was a game for older children because it involved an element of danger. It was usually played around stages and flakes. Home was a spot marked out on the beach.

The hiding places were behind puncheons, on the roofs of the stages, under sunken wharves and in empty tanpots.

Hide and Seek took in quite an area and to reach Home without being tagged, you'd have to dodge newly-painted dories, tubs of baited handlines and stacked lobster pots. If we were discovered playing in forbidden territory, someone's father would shout "Get the hell home, you bunch of devilskins," and as fast as we could go, we went.

* * *

On the western side of the Cove, a line of jagged boulders provided a margin of shelter for the small boats moored on the collar. On calm days in the summer, we clambered out there and lay on our stomachs to watch the connors and sculpins dart in and out of the cabbage kelp that grew in thick brown bunches near the base of the boulders.

We teased the connors to the surface by dipping our toes in the water and when they came uncomfortably close, splashed with our feet to send them scurrying helter skelter to safety in the shadows of the reef.

The Salmon Hole

The stream that flowed through St. Leonard's was called the Brook. Fed by the waters of ponds, a few miles inland, it snaked through marshes where bakeapples blossomed white in the warmth of the June sun. It slittered through waist-high bracken in the swampland of the lower levels before dashing recklessly into the narrow ravine that directed its course through the village and into the sea.

Centuries of tumbling waters had gouged a basin under a shelf of rocks forming an ideal spot to bathe all summer long. It was called the Salmon Hole.

We went there, three or four times a day, creeping barefoot along the sloping shale bank where hosts of devil's darn' needles twirled and dived above our heads as they scanned the quiet pools and plots of flag flowers for unwary water flies. We thought they were intent only on sticking their needles in our hair, and we marched single file, with our towels wrapped around our heads, to the safety of higher ground and the sun-splashed water of the Salmon Hole

When spring rains
tumbled the waters brown
and the brook ran higher
than the alder tree
that marked the pool
we worried and hoped
the flow would slack by June.

All spring long
we made impatient trips
to measure with sticks
how fast the water leapt
pool by pool to the sea
below.

Then one day
in the warmth of the sun
we undressed and tip-toed
into the swirling foam
at the pool's edge
and holding on to each other's hands
we waded laughing
into one more summer.

An Economical Lot

Obviously, the early settlers were an economical lot, as is evident in the methods that were used to prepare and distribute food, especially livestock and fish. Every edible part of an animal or fish was preserved to last through the seasons when these items became scarce or were impossible to obtain. For example:

The stomach tissue of beef animals were salted and prepared for meals as tripe.

The hard dry fat was preserved as suet.

Other types of fat were rendered for lard.

The head was made into head cheese.

The tongue was preserved by salting.

The heart, liver and lights were used as required by the housewife for meals of her choice.

The tail was skinned and cut into lengths for soup.

Intestines and blood were used to make blood puddings.

The skin was tanned to use for leather.

The hocks were used in the preparation of glue.

The horns were made into powder-horns.

There was hardly any end to ingenuity in those days.

Monday's Child

Monday's child is fair of face.
Tuesday's child is full of grace.
Wednesday's child is full of woe.
Thursday's child has far to go.
Friday's child is loving and giving.
Saturday's child works hard for its living.
But the child that is born on the Sabbath day,
Is bright and merry, good and gay.

Seven Crows

One for sorrow
Two for joy
Three for a wedding
Four for a boy
Five for silver
Six for gold
Seven for a secret never told

Settler's Remedies

To cure white mouth in infants
    brush with the white lining of the marsh rush.

To stop bleeding of a finger
    apply pressure with the leaf of the Virgin flower.

To stop nosebleeds
    place a cold stone on the nape of the neck.

To remove splinters
    bandage with a paste made from soap and molasses.

To cure skin infections
    bake hot bread poultices.

Sasafras tea cures stomach cramps.

Drink a mixture of lime (slacked) and water
    to give you healthy bones.

Drink a mixture of sulphur and molasses
    to cleanse the blood.

Purgative drugs — Senna tea, Castor oil and Epsom salts.

Apply bags of hot salt for strained muscles.

Wear brass chains for infections caused
    by friction of oilskin cuffs on fishermen's wrists.

Pour black rum on an aching tooth.

Apply a scale of tobacco to cuts from a razor.

Control excessive bleeding with cobwebs.

Heal flesh wounds with turpentine from a fir tree.

To cure rheumatism wear a potato.

To cure aching legs bathe in sea water.

Apply bandages, soaked in vinegar to swollen joints.

Cure warts by counting the number
    then marking the same number of X s
    on the back of the stove. When the marks burn off
    the warts will have disappeared.

Rub a sty with a gold wedding ring.

Goin' In The Country

Every winter about the middle of January, the men arranged a hunting trip to the foothills of the Tolt. The Tolt is a small mountain about thirty miles inland from the mouth of Sandy Harbour river.

The trail led through thick woods, across rivers and over tricky marshes. Fortunately, the St. Leonard's men had the advantage of using a dogteam belonging to a man in Davis Cove, because a couple of men from that community were always included in the party that made the annual trip.

The first part of this journey began at St. Leonard's. The men put all their gear in a dory and rowed around twenty-five miles to Davis Cove where they met up with the other hunters.

The main purpose of the trip was to hunt caribou, and the area around Wigwam Brook, where a campsite had been chosen, was believed to have been the hunting grounds of the Red Indian. This was wonderful rabbit country too, so that a successful hunt could, and often did, result in three or four caribou, thirty or forty braces of rabbits and a couple of dozen partridges.

The trip was referred to as "a deer hunt to shoot caribou to get venison for the winter."

The men travelled as lightly as possible, taking the bare necessities; a canvas tent, a small campstove made of tin, a tin of kerosene oil, a few tallow candles, several pair of sheep's wool socks, an extra pair of homespun drawers, woolen mitts and a country cap.

Each hunter was equipped with a gun and powder-horn together with enough gunshot and oakum required for the week's hunt. One man in the party took an axe and each man took his shavin' knife, pipe, Jumbo tobacco and matches.

The women prepared the food and added other necessary items: a tin kettle and an enamel pot , some strips of clean white cloth to use for bandages in case of an accident, a sewing needle and some thread, spoons and forks. There were batches of country buns and loaves of soda bread, allowing so many a day and a few extra just in case, a pound or so of flour, baking soda, a piece of fatback pork, tea, salt and molasses. All this was put in a gunny sack.

Arriving at Wigwam Brook, the men would set up camp. This was the base from which they would hunt the caribou during daylight and to which they'd return each evening. It was here they set rabbit slips for the convenience of checking them morning and evening, and here too they'd be able to shoot the partridge that flocked to feed on brouse that grew in clumps a short distance from camp.

There were no means of communicating with the hunters from the day they left St. Leonard's until their return, so the wives and relatives went about their daily tasks, often stopping to chat with each other about the kind of weather the men might be having in the country. When the time drew near for the hunters to come back, the men at home took turns climbing to the lookout until the dory was sighted. Then everyone gathered on the beach to welcome the hunters home.

Once it was known that they were all well, the women hurried back to the kitchens to get a hot meal ready and lay out clean shifts. Plenty of water was heated and made ready for washing and shaving.

Neighbors helped to unload the dory and asked about the trip in general. They'd get all the details later some night when the trip would be told and retold in neighbors' kitchens where the men gathered on winter nights. On such nights the kitchen became a stage where each man re-enacted his own participation in the hunt.

Old men, great hunters in their day, listened, refilled their pipes, and waited to taste,once again, the meal of venison stewing on the big Waterloo stove.

The old timers were not to be outdone by the yarns of the younger men. On one occasion I listened to an eighty year old resident recount a trip in the country.

I 'members, t'wus one of the coldest winters I seen in my time. T'wus late in the evenin' when we reached Wigwam Brook and t'wus too damn cold to make camp. So, we made up our minds to bed down as best we could until mornin'.

The dogs were hungry and barkin' somethin' fierce. Paddy went off into the bushes to shoot a couple of rabbits to feed to the dogs. By 'n bye, he comes back, holdin' out his gun with his fingers froze to the lock. That's how cold t'wus.

Anyways, we got to work and cut enough brush to make a circle of boughs in a small clearin'. We hauled our gear inside which wus about fifteen or thereabouts feet in diameter. Then we sprayed some kerosene oil on the boughs and set fire to 'em.

When the turpentine caught, up she went. The sparks flew and the fire roared. We didn't want to unpack for fear there wouldn't be a lull in the weather and then we wouldn't be able to get on the barrens to get our caribou. So then, we sat on some boughs and drank what rum we had. We had to nap in turns because we had to keep puttin' brush on the fire to make heat enough to keep ourselves from freezin' to death.

By daylight we knew the best thing to do wus to go back to Sandy Harbour river and do some rabbit catchin'. So we took the dogsleds, loaded on our gear and started back.

We couldn't douse the fire 'cause the ice, my son, was a foot thick in the brook. Our mitts were froze as hard as the hobs o' hell and our grub brags were froze to the sleds.

When we reached Sandy Harbour river, we set up camp and spent a spell rabbit catchin'. When we had twenty or thirty brace, we headed for home. Our grub wus low and we fear'd the women would be concerned. We reached Davis Cove one evenin' just at dark. Billy Hynes, Billy wus with us that trip, unharnessed his dogs and we got ready to row up to St. Leonard's the next mornin'.

We didn't think much of the trip. We had no caribou and done no huntin' at all but t'wus early in the winter and we planned another smack at her if the weather let up any.

Well sir, we never did get back to hunt that winter. But around the first week of July, a crew came down from Canada to do some prospectin' for cuttin' pit-props inside of Sandy Harbour river. Sure enough, they came upon the spot where we lit the fire and it wusn't long before the news spread that them prospectors had found gold right on the ground in by Wigwam Brook. Now that wus somethin'.

When they got the experts in to see what they were goin' to do about the gold mine, that crowd discovered what the prospectors tought wus gold, wus only the frozen flames of the fire we lit to keep ourselves from freezin' to death that night at Wigwam Brook. Now how cold do you think it wus that winter, I wonder, when even the fire froze so hard it wusn't even melted come July.

And that's the God's truth, too.

Verse

Written by Sister Cornelia Sullivan as a child in St. Leonard's, and found in her father's strongbox after his death.

The Fairy Fountain

I know of a fairy fountain,
Among the moss and fern,
In the fairies' magic garden
At the white road's graceful turn.

Close to the fairy fountain,
Is my fairy palace of dreams,
In the heart of the murmuring spruces
And the midst of the bubbling streams.

The fairies dance in the moonlight
On the margin of the lake.
I know, for the whispering birches
Tell secrets when I wake.

And on the moss and fern leaves
There are footprints everywhere,
And once I found, but please don't tell,
A strand of golden hair.

* * *

Written by Mrs. Annie Brennan, and found in her dictionary after her death.

St. Leonard's, my dear old home,
Deserted and forlorn,
The people forced to leave it,
With no choice of their own.

The verdant fields,
The wooded hills
Still are left unharmed.
The beauty that God gave them
Still retains its charm.

Our fathers and forefathers
Lie in their peaceful sleep,
While birds hover around them,
Their silent watch to keep.

Good-bye, good-bye, St. Leonard's,
Good-bye, good-bye forever.
That ties that bind me to my home,
Naught but death can sever.

* * *

My First Recitation

Grade Two

I once had a sweet little doll, dears
The prettiest doll in the world.
Her cheeks were so red and so white, dears
And her hair was so prettily curled.

I lost my poor little doll, dears
As I played in the field one day.
I searched for her more than a week, dears
But I never could find where she lay.

I found my poor little doll, dears
As I played in the field one day.
Her clothes were all tattered and torn, dears
And her paint was all washed away.

Her arm trodden off by the cows, dears
And her hair not the least bit curled.
But she is still to me, dears
The prettiest doll in the world.

St. Leonard's

The following is an excerpt, reproduced in form from the original, from the late Archbishop Howley's "Newfoundland Name-Lore" which appeared in the *Newfoundland Quarterly* commencing October 1901. It was subsequently reprinted in *The Little Nord Easter: Reminiscences of a Placentia Bayman* by Victor Butler, edited by Wilfred Wareham, Canada's Atlantic Folklore/Folklife Series, Breakwater Books Ltd. (St. John's, 1980)

There is a little cove called
St.Leonard's
to the westward of Isle Valen. It appears to be so called from the name of a family of settlers of whom survivors still remain. In olden times this place was called
Oliver's Cove
but when the late Venerable Parish Priest — Rev. Father James Walsh — removed from his residence in Merasheen, somewhere towards the middle of the XIX Century, about 1850, to the little cove or arm at the bottom of Presque Inlet; being of strenuous old Keltic stock, he could not bear the name of Oliver, as it reminded him too much of "Crummle," so he changed the name to
St.Kyran's
the Patron Saint of his native County of Kilkenny. The place is somewhat lonely, being situated in a secluded glen at the end of the Northern Arm of Presque. This arm of the sea is entirely surrounded by high wooded mountains and closed in, except a very narrow entrance opposite Presque. The mountains are covered up to their summits with rich growth of foliage. The scenery is strikingly like one of the salt water locks of Scotland, such as the Garlock, Lock Long, Lock Eil, &c. The Presbytery is built upon

a little peninsula jutting out into the lake and is a most charming and picturesque spot. The fruit and flower gardens, owing to the care and skill of the present Pastor — Rev. Father Doutney — and his energetic and tasteful household, are some of the most beautiful and flourishing in Newfoundland.

The Rev. Fr. Walsh was nearer than perhaps he thought in connecting the name of Oliver's Cove with Oliver Cromwell. We find as far back as 1696, the Abbe Baudouin describing the marching of the French troops after the capture of St. John's says that having marched round Conception Bay they attacked without capturing — Carbonear Island. They marched to Heart's Content and round the shores of Trinity Bay to Chapel Arm; crossed over the Isthmus of Avalon into Placentia Bay, then: "On the 19th of March, M. D'Ibberville left Placentia in a boat for the

Bay of Cromwell.

Here they met with M. Peiriere who came from Bay Bulls' Arm to meet them. This is undoubtedly Oliver's Cove, however it came by the name.

Typical Old-Time Newfoundland Kitchen
from **The Newfoundland Quarterly** Summer Number 1944

I first heard The Silvery Tide *sung by Joe Green from Davis Cove in June of 1924. He had shipped out to John Joe Leonard for the caplin skull that year and it was in John Joe's house in St.Leonard's one Sunday evening I heard the song for the first time. It's been one of my favourites ever since. Typical of the kind of song you'd most likely hear at that time in St. Leonard's and places like it, it was sung without musical accompaniment, told a story, and was a lot longer than the songs you hear going around nowadays.*

The Silvery Tide

Down by the rolling ocean there slept a damsel fair
She was comely tall and handsome, she was called the village dear
Her heart she gave to a young man, far on the ocean wide
And true she was to young Henry who's on the silvery tide.

Young Henry long being absent, a nobleman there came
A-courting pretty Mary, but she refused the same
I pray begone, there is but one, there is but one she cried
And I pray begone, there is only one and he's on the silvery tide.

This nobleman in a passion, those words to her did say
To prove your separation, I will take your life away
I will watch you late and early, till you alone I'll spy
And you'll sink or swim far far from him who's on the silvery tide.

This nobleman was walking one evening to take the air
Down by the rolling ocean, he spied this damsel fair
Now said that cruel villain, consent and be my bride
Or you'll sink or swim far far from him who's on the silvery tide.

Oh no, oh no, dear sir she said, my vows I dare not break
Oh no, oh no, said Mary, I will die for his sweet sake
He took a pocket handkerchief, her tender hands he tied
And while screaming she went floating out on the silvery tide.

It happened not long after, young Henry returned from sea
Expecting to be married and appoint his wedding day
Your own true love has been murdered, her aged parents cried
She has proven her own destruction, down on the silvery tide.

Young Henry went to bed that night, but no rest could he find
For thoughts of pretty Mary kept running through his mind
He dreamt that he was sailing far on the ocean wide
And his true love she sat weeping down by the silvery tide.

Young Henry arose at midnight to search those seabanks ov'r
From three o'clock in the morning he wandered from shore to shore
Til four o'clock in the evening a lifeless body he spied
Which to and fro'came floating, out on the silvery tide.

He knew that it was his own true love by the gold ring on her hand
He unfastened that pocket handkerchief that brought him to a stand
The name of that cruel villain, young Henry quickly spied
That put an end to Mary, down on the silvery tide.

This nobleman was taken, the gallows was his doom
For murdering pretty Mary all in her youthful bloom
Young Henry quite distracted, he wandered until he died
And his last words were "poor Mary down on the silvery tide."

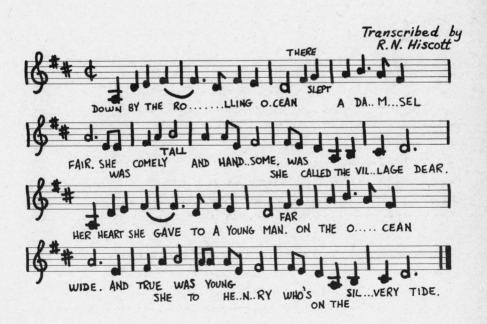

The Church of the Assumption and the priest's house in ruins (May 1978)

The Priest's root cellar

The Road

The Road was constructed to connect St. Leonard's to the neighbouring outport of St. Kyrans. Wide, blue-graveled and with wooden bridges spanning the brooks, it led to the church, the school and the post office. When the stone church, which was situated between the two settlements, was destroyed by fire in 1921, the new church of the Assumption was built adjacent to the presbytery and facing the harbour of St. Kyran's. The Road was bordered on one side by hills covered in thick stands of spruce, fir and birch trees and on the other by cultivated fields, the Chapel Pond and stretches of pasture land. It wound through a valley that was historical in landmarks and shrines born of the romance and superstition of the early Irish settlers.

The first place of interest to us, as children was Mr. Igg's raspberry patch. He really didn't care about the raspberries, they just happened to grow around a pile of rocks accumulated in the process of clearing the land in his grandfather's time. Nevertheless, he resented anyone, much less a crowd of youngsters, tramping through his meadow. A crowd, to him, meant as few as two or three. The gate was always tied and we knew full well that he inspected the knots, but we knew where a picket was loose on the bottom rail some distance from the gate. We would squeeze through the small opening and squirm on our stomachs to the pile of rocks. Once there, we were sheltered by the tall raspberry bushes. We took turns standing guard, in case Mr. Igg took a notion to mow some hay or take a suspicious stroll to his garden. In any case, we would have time to make a fast retreat to the picket hole and wriggle out to safety on the road.

The Road in May 1978

LIZA'S ROCK

Then there was Liza's Rock. This was at the lower end of Chapel Pond which bordered the road for about half a mile. We always took a rest here and conjured up terrible stories about Liza. We were told never to ask questions about the woman the rock was called after, but the people spoke of her as 'poor Liza' and of strange noises heard late in the evening and at night. The old people warned us to say a prayer for her soul when we passed the rock on our way to school and we would, because it was a good place to take a spell in broad daylight.

A little farther on was the Violet Mash. To get at the flowers we had to kick off our shoes because the biggest violets grew in the wettest places almost covered in the lush grasses where a small brook dribbled from the slope of the hill. We waded in the grass and picked handfuls for ourselves and likely as not a few for Aunt Aidy, who was no relation. Everyone called her Aunt Aidy and we always brought her wild flowers to put in a vase in front of the picture of her son with his officer's uniform on and who had served in the British Navy during World War I.

Then the Scrape. It was a bit dangerous here and we were often warned about it, but this was where the biggest and bluest harebells grew, apart from the ones we could not possibly get at, high in the cliff over the fish stages. If you were really expert in clinging to the overhanging roots of old spruce, you could gather a handful of googs that ripened on the bunches of maiden-hair close to the edge of the Scrape. This was also a great place to collect rocks, uncovered in the Spring thaw. The peculiar shapes and colours of the rocks were fascinating and we often brought some to school, especially the ones full of 'fools' gold.'

Lodore was the most fascinating place. We were good for a couple of hours here, especially after a heavy rainfall. The water fell one hundred feet straight down from a narrow gorge and the roar of the falls could be heard long before Lodore came into view. It was far enough off the Road to afford a bit of privacy and often we undressed and bathed in the pools, standing under the spray where the water dashed from the slate cliff-side. If we squeezed in far enough, the water went over us in a white curve, only the mist touching our bodies where the sunlight came through. We called it the rainbow room.

A short distance from Lodore were the ruins of the old stone church where we were not ever supposed to go, but where we went anyway. The stone walls and curved windows threw the sound of our voices back at us in countless repetitions and we made ourselves hoarse shouting "echo, echo, echo," listening to the words roll away in the hillside until there was no sound at all. We made sure we got out of there before the sun went down because of ghosts, especially the "two black dogs with no heads" that walked through the churchyard gate between daylight and dark, and vanished in front of your eyes. On the other hand, we would have welcomed the sound of the Sanctus bell that the old people said they had heard on Sunday mornings for months after the church was destroyed by fire.

Directly across the Road from the Old Church was the belfry. The door had no lock, so we often took shelter there from a summer shower. It was built similar to the shape of a lighthouse tower, supported by a stone base. The sexton's chair served as a platform on which we stood to sing songs or recite while we waited for the rain to stop. In the thick mossy soil behind the belfry, we picked Mayflowers for our May altars. Besides having a May altar in the church and one in the school, we each had one at home. We needed an awful lot of Mayflowers to decorate all the altars. It wouldn't do to have the Blessed Virgin neglected in any one place.

Father Walsh's Well

There was a well a short distance from the ruins of the Old Church. It was called Father Walsh's Well, and was built by the masons who were doing the work on the church at that time. It was built over a spring and the roof was curved concrete with a small stone cross in the center. No one ever passed by without stopping to take a sip of the cold spring water. It not only kept away the evil spirits, but also helped to quench the thirst on a hot summer day. Bordered by tall trees, it served as a landmark, a shrine and a resting place. There was always a dipper to use, but it was more fun to kneel on the stones and scoop the water up with cupped hands, or bend over and slurp the water with your mouth. The water was always cold, so cold it made your teeth pain.

The Well

We sat talking
watching the water flow
over the flagstones
sipped it cold and clear
from the dented dipper
with the wooden handle
and could have stayed
all day if they hadn't been waiting
for water at home

as it was we lingered
as long as we could
until at last
we splashed our buckets full
and hurried wet-legged
over the meadow and out the road
leaving our rippling reflections
to settle and fade
in the fond fountain of our youth

Just beyond the Well, the Graveyard Road began. In the day time, it was a grassy avenue where twin-flowers grew in abundance and sparrows built their nests in stands of young spruce near the side of it. In the shadows of evening, it became a demon's cavern, where banshees screamed and wierd forms leapt to the swish of the wind in the tall timber, and the headstones appeared like a procession of ghosts lining up for their nightly rituals. We were not allowed to use the graveyard as a playground and only went there with older people to set flowers on the graves or help paint the fence on family plots.

The Pond Field got its name from its close proximity to the Chapel Pond, though the original name of the pond was Lake St. Peter and Paul, no doubt so-called in honour of the sculptured images on either side of the front door of the church built in 1856. The field was enclosed by a wire fence and was church property. It contained about eight acres of cleared land, used for growing hay except during the early fall, when cattle were put to pasture. A shoal brook meandered near the edge of the field away from the Road and out of sight of people passing. In spring, we waded in the brook when swathes of snow still lingered in the hill and the pussy willows dipped mischievously from the alder tips. Later, when the sun warmed the valley and the posies turned yellow in the new grass, we made chains from the stalks to wear on our necks. When the grass was higher and blowing white with wild daisies, we collected armloads and sat under the trees plucking the petals and repeating the words of "the daisy fortune teller."

What will my husband be? Rich man, poor man, beggar man, thief, doctor, lawyer, Indian chief.
Does he love me? He do, he don't, a little, not much, sincere to the heart, none at all.
When shall I marry? This year, next year, now or never.
What shall I wear at my wedding? Silk, satin, calico, rags.
Where shall I live? In a little house, big house, pigsty, barn.

With so many petals to pluck, each of us had a fairly good chance of marrying a rich man who loved us and lived in a big house. We would surely wear a satin dress, but sadly enough would have to wait to grow up for all this to happen.

The Hollow of Mrs. Dunn's was where the Road dipped slightly to a straight stretch of five or six hundred feet before ending at the Green Gates and the entrance to the priest's residence. The original site of Mrs. Dunn's house was on a knoll close to where the Carriage Road branched off from the main road. The Carriage Road was so-called because it led to the parish stables in St. Kyran's. A coach and pair was used to transport the priest and his relatives to the church on Sundays in the summertime, but this custom ended when Rev. Dean Doutney was transferred to another parish in 1913. This junction was referred to as the 'turnstile' by many of the old residents for reasons we did not know.

The Hollow was an enchanting stretch of the Road for us on our way to and from school. We'd always stop here where a wooden sluice carried the water under the road from a source unknown to us. There was a bare trickle at this point, but we could hear the gurgling of water over stones somewhere near and inside the wire fence of the priest's property. Many of our pastimes were pursued in forbidden territory, but we had to consider that going through the priest's fence might involve something more than "a talking to" from our parents.

Nevertheless, one evening, near the end of June, we hid our schoolbags and crawled through the fence. Just a few yards from where we entered under a canopy of young birch and alder, was a small mossy dell with a bubbling brook. Shafts of sunlight splintered through the trees, Jack-in-the-pulpits and June flowers like miniature stars, dotted the edge of the pool. The place was as magic as could be and we called it the Fairy Dell and kept its location a secret for all of that long long-ago summer.

The road to The Green Gates

Christmas in the Cove

The Christmas season held great religious significance for the residents of St. Leonard's. Before preparing for the social events of the Twelve Days, the men decorated the church with evergreens and built a platform in the sanctuary where the Crib would be on display for all of the twelve days.

The stable was made by a local carpenter who worked at the priest's place. It was made of small fir logs, no bigger than pickets. The roof was covered with birch bark and the floor was strewn with straw. The figures were large and lifelike. Every time we went to church during Christmas, we visited the Crib and dropped money in a small box set nearby in commemoration of the gifts of the Magi.

Everyone who was able went to confession on Christmas Eve and attended midnight mass or the mass on Christmas Day. In those years Christmas Eve was considered a fast day by the church and the meals were made from various kinds of fish and vegetables. This fast before feast whetted the appetite so that Christmas Day dinner was appreciated all the more.

Christmas trees were introduced to the area in the last of the 1800s. Each family would have a tree set up in the parlour, or in the kitchen, which in outport houses, was the largest and warmest room. There would be garlands of small fir boughs tied together and draped around the ceiling and hung over the windows. Christmas cards, kept year after year, were displayed around the room and placed on the branches of the tree. Every year, a bright shiny five-point star was made from tin for the tree top. Paper bells, strings of figs and bright red berries were hung on the tips of the branches. Apples were also used as tree decorations and attached with coloured yarns. Later on, in the early 1900s, a catalogue from the business firm of Ayre & Sons in St. John's was distributed to homeowners in St. Leonard's, introducing them to the sophisticated baubles and tinsel garlands which were available by mail order.

Because the traditional revelry of the twelve days was related, for the most part, to the grown-ups, the children were well-provided with things to delight them on Christmas morning and to amuse them during the stormy days of a long and dreary winter.

Fathers and grandfathers were expert carpenters and secretly began making toys, long before the Christmas season arrived. This work was done in the store lofts in the daytime and in the comfort of the kitchens at night when the children were in bed. There was quite a variety of wooden toys made in those days and all of them were interesting as well as durable. A favourite toy for little boys was the slug gun, a miniature replica of the "long tom" with a cotton drawstring bag, full of half inch slugs for ammunition. Spin tops, whittled with care and precision were painted in bright colours. There might be a swing for the baby made from hardwood slats and empty thread spools. There'd be games of Fox and Geese, wooden animals, little chairs, and dolls' cradles, and there'd always be knitted stockings, caps, scarves, sweaters, vamps, and fancy mitts. And there might be a novelty gift of some kind purchased during the summer or brought from St. Peter's in the fall and hidden away until everything was assembled for distribution on Christmas Eve. These gifts were things like hair ribbons, lace handkerchiefs, necklaces and scented soaps.

The small gifts were put in the stockings with bunches of figs, apples and sweets. The big presents were never wrapped nor put under the tree. They were laid near the stove or on the settle where St. Nick was supposed to leave them.

The older members of the family did not receive presents but usually wore a new garment and dressed in their Sunday best more often than any other time of the year.

Christmas dinner was a special family get-together. The best of the garden produce was kept in the root cellar for this occasion. The meal was one of roast beef, rabbit, or seabirds, served with salt beef, cabbage, turnip, carrots, parsnips and potatoes, figgy duff and peas pudding. Steamed suet pudding was served with rum sauce as a dessert.

The afternoon of Christmas Day was spent visiting relatives and neighbours. The children visited each other and compared gifts.

The custom of mummering at Christmas time was highlighted by a display of local talent. The mummers, dressed in all kinds of fancy attire, began to visit the houses after supper on Christmas night. The older people went in a group while the younger boys and girls usually formed their own party. Sometimes people came from nearby settlements to join the others.

As this was the only time during the year that the fishermen could relax and enjoy themselves, they began preparations in early fall when the first boat left for St. Peter's with a load of birch billets to be bartered for coarse salt, hip rubbers, oilskins and enough contraband rum to celebrate the twelve days of Christmas.

As the mummers went from door to door, they were invited to enter and entertain by singing, dancing and playing their musical instruments.

Those who could not sing recited poetry and acted out humorous skits to the delight of everyone.

The ordinary chores were attended to during the day so that the events of each night of the twelve could be enjoyed in the companionship of relatives and neighbours. The festivities ended on Old Christmas Day with a soup supper and dance in the parish hall at St. Kyran's.

January

Once Old Christmas Day was past and gone, the Cove settled in to cope with the vagrant weather of the longest and coldest month of the year. Even the hills seemed to pull themselves together to shelter the Cove from the stinging blasts of a sudden nord'easter or the biting whips of a gusty west wind.

The heavy snowdrifts cemented the motor boats and rodneys to the beach where they were hauled up above highwater mark.

A few dories were left in readiness, to launch for turr hunting and to coast loads of firewood, fencing rails and pickets for use in the spring.

While the wind moaned in the door jambs and slashed at everything in its path, the men of the Cove gathered in their store-lofts in the afternoons knitting twine. "Knittin' twine" referred to all the work involved in making and repairing fishing gear; making cod traps and cod nets, replacing lobster pot heads and seines, in preparation for the fishery the following summer.

On such afternoons, the old skippers ambled to the lofts to sit and criticize or praise, according to their moods, while the less industrious fed birch junks to the bogie and sat on mounds of discarded gear as they listened to the sea-talk about the first trip to the White Sail, or the summers spent in Golden Bay.

The smell of bark and oakum rose from hidden corners, and glass floats blinked green in the light of the flames from the stove.

When evening wore on, the smell of kerosene oil from the lantern mingled with tobacco smoke and the muted, spasmodic conversation of the old skippers waned as the daylight disappeared in the dark waters of the Cove.

The women fretted around their kitchens, washing and cooking. They fed the hens and coaxed the truant ducks from the open stretches of water in the pond.

The youngsters helped, as much as they were able to ease the burden of domestic tasks. Every evening there were splits to be chopped for morning fires and woodboxes to be filled, water to be brought bucket by bucket from the spring well, and brouse to be gathered from the nearby woods to supplement the diets of sheep and goats.

When the lamps were lit in the kitchens and the last shed door was slammed shut, the men hung up their twine needles, picked up their caps and pipes, turned the big wooden buttons on the store-loft doors, and took the paths that led to the comfort of their kitchens where the smell of hot soup and freshly-baked bread rose like steam, warm and welcome, from the Waterloo stove.

Let the winds scream and the snowdrifts swirl. The outdoor elements would not enter the cozy kitchens tonight, and tomorrow would be time enough to deal with any inconvenience a January night may have splattered on the little outport.

April

It is April. Backyard fences are draped with brightly-coloured hooked mats. Clothes lines are strung with patchwork quilts and cushion covers. Every window is raised to rid the houses of winter odours.

The neighbours call to each other from open doorways and there is a constant procession of housewives going to the spring well, where they chat about their plans for spring cleaning and relate news of relatives and friends they corresponded with during the winter.

Grandmother sits in her rocking chair near the door where the sunlight slants warm on her aged face.

Grandfather walks down the lane to the landwash where the men are busy repairing mooring ropes and lobster traps. He scans the wharves and stages to see how much damage winter's Nord Easters did. He sees a broken strouter, a few missing longers, and reminds the younger men to have a look-out for good sticks the next time they go in the droke. He sniffs the warm south wind and wishes he was young again, but he knows only too well that the boats will skid into the water without his help this spring. He'll be lucky if they'll let him keep the fires going under the tan pots. The distance from the beach to the woodpile seems a lot more than it used to be. And there's Grandmother up there not wanting him to do anything at all hardly. But he'll get his punt out that's one thing certain. He'll 'cork' her and paint her and put her out on the collar. He mightn't use her at all, mightn't even get out for a row, but at least she'll be out there on the water where she belongs. She's a good punt yet and he won't let her dry up on the beach. No sir. It's April already and soon enough now it'll be summer, and all hands will be at the fish again. Grandfather won't be at it with them but what odds now that it's April, and the ice is melting and the weather is warming up. It's a good time to be alive anyway, even for Grandfather. Especially for Grandfather.

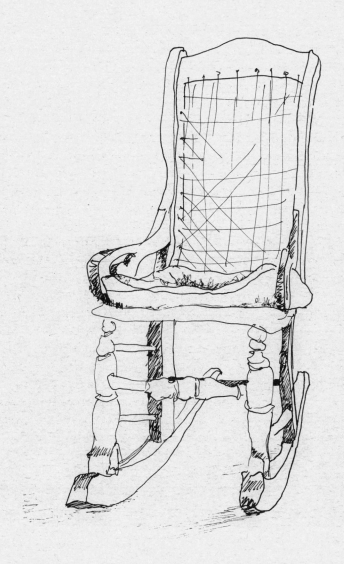

The recipes contained in this volume are not intended to make up a comprehensive collection of any kind. They are, simply, the recipes I recall being used in the homes of St. Leonard's when I lived there, first as a youngster in my mother's house, and later as a young woman keeping my own kitchen and feeding my own family.

L.M.

In days gone by the handiest measuring utensil in the kitchen was the palm of the hand, and often, if you borrowed a recipe, the list of ingredients would include "a dash of this" and "a smidgen of that" or "enough to taste," and somehow the amounts and the methods were always foolproof.

Fish and a Few Accompaniments

Boiled Mussels

mussels
salt water
kelp
butter
pepper

Shellfish are affected by the moon's growth. Therefore, the best time to pick mussels is during the first quarter or when the moon is full.

Take advantage of a calm evening when the tide is low. Grab a bucket and a garden rake and find yourself a mussel bed. Close to shore the mussels will be of the blue variety — the horse mussel which is much larger, but not near so tasty as the blue mussel, is found in deeper water.

Rake the mussels loose from their clutch on the shoal. Work quickly because mussels, like all shellfish, hold their flavour better when cooked as soon as possible after gathering.

Douse some sea water over the mussels and strain them to get rid of excess sand. Gather some wet kelp and head for the fire.

Pack the mussels in a large iron boiler with layers of kelp. Fill with salt water and cover.

Build a fire outdoors in preference to using the kitchen stove. The smell of boiling kelp is not very appetizing.

Put the boiler on the fire and let the mussels boil rapidly for 25 to 30 minutes. Strain off the water and remove the kelp. Discard any mussels that have remained closed. Shell the remainder and remove the whiskers and sand sacs.

Place the mussels in a heated serving dish, add melted butter and a sprinkling of pepper and serve. You may also serve them in the shell and let each person season them to his own taste.

In St. Leonard's the mussel shells were smashed with a hammer and fed to the hens or thrown in the cabbage bed along with the kelp.

Roasted Scrawd

*Scrawds were small cod culled from catches of trap fish. They had
no market value because of their size but were preserved by light
salting for use at home in the early part of the summer. After a
few days under salt, they were washed and spread on the flake to
dry in the sun for a day or two.*

To prepare for serving, water a whole scrawd in cold water for five or
six hours. Take it from the water and wipe it dry with a cup towel.

Wrap the scrawd in three or four layers of brown paper and fold the
edges in firmly.

Place the package on a wood fire and pull the burning embers around
and over it.

When the paper is charred all over, remove it from the fire and peel the
layers of burnt paper from the scrawd. The contents should be golden
brown and moist.

Serve roasted scrawd with hot tea, homemade bread, and fresh butter
for breakfast, supper, or late-night mug-up.

Fried Cod Roe

This is a simple recipe and was usually served as a breakfast meal to the men before they went out to tend their cod traps. The roe was cooked the night before and took only a short time to dish up in the morning.

Choose medium roe from fresh codfish. Boil slowly in salted water for thirty minutes. Remove the roe from the water, drain it, and allow it to cool.

Fry several rashers of salt pork until crisp. Remove the rashers and keep them hot.

Slice the roe and dip each slice into the following mixture:

> 1 cup of grated breadcrumbs
> ½ cup of milk
> 1 beaten egg
> ½ tsp of salt
> ¼ tsp of pepper.

Fry each slice in pork fat until browned on both sides and serve with hot rashers.

Toast and Fish

Toast and fish was usually made from left-over salt cod but you can start from scratch if you like. It is especially good if you're in the country hunting or trouting. You may prepare the sauce at home or cook it on the spot. Toast the bread on an alder stick over hot coals and wash down the meal with a mug of hot tea.

If you have no left-over salt fish in the house, remove the skin from a salt cod and water overnight. Put the fish in a pot of cold water and bring to a boil. Let it simmer for thirty minutes or so until the fish is done.

Make a white sauce by mixing:

3 tbsp of flour
3 tbsp of butter

Blend well and add:

½ cup of chopped onion
enough boiling water to form a smooth sauce

Stir well to keep the sauce free from lumps. Add salt to taste and a dash of pepper. Keep the sauce hot but do not allow to boil.

Put the cooked fish on a platter and remove all the bones. Flake with a fork, add to the sauce and stir.

Butter slices of homemade bread and place in a hot oven until the butter melts and the bread browns slightly.

Pour the hot fish sauce over the toast and serve.

Fish and Brewis

A simple and delicious meal, fish and brewis is still a favourite dish in many Newfoundland households. The brewis is actually a hard bread commonly called "hard tack." It is readily available in stores in Newfoundland.

To prepare fish and brewis you will need:

> 1 medium salt codfish
> ½ pound of salt pork
> 5 cakes of hard bread
> ½ tsp of salt

Cut or tear the fish into several pieces and soak in cold water overnight. Break the hard bread in pieces and soak in cold water overnight in a separate pot.

Next day strain the water from the fish and add fresh water to cover. Boil the fish until tender. Remove the skin and large bones.

About ten minutes before the fish is cooked, put the hard bread in a pot using the same water it was soaked in. Add 1 teaspoon of salt, boil quickly, and strain.

To make scruncheons, cut the salt pork into small cubes and fry until they are rendered of fat and golden brown.

Place portions of fish on hot plates. Spoon brewis on the side and sprinkle fish and brewis with hot fat and scruncheons.

Boiled Lobster

live lobsters
cold water
salt

Half fill a large boiler with cold water and add ¼ cup of coarse salt. Bring the water to a rapid boil. Plunge the lobsters head first into the boiling water and let them boil vigorously for 30 minutes. When the lobsters are done, the shell should be a bright red colour and the tails curled close to the body. Remove the lobsters from the water and allow them to cool some before serving. Shell the lobsters and serve them with potatoes and cold dressing.

The tail and claws provide the white solid meat, but there are other succulent tidbits in the body of a lobster that may be served in a separate dish.

The lobster cheese which is clustered behind the "old woman" in the body section and the sweet tasting green tissue that clings to the inside of the shell are delicious and too often discarded.

The "old woman" (a marine biologist might call it by another name) is not to be eaten. I don't know what injury it will do you but we were always told it was "poison."

Drawn Butter

Drawn butter is a creamy sauce that goes well with any salt fish recipe.

To make drawn butter you will need:

¼ cup of milk
2 tbsp of butter
3 tbsp of flour
salt to taste
¼ cup of chopped onion
boiling water

Melt butter in a saucepan and mix in the flour. Add the milk and stir well. Add salt and onion. Stirring constantly, pour enough boiling water on the mixture to give it a light liquid texture. Put the saucepan on the stove and cook until the drawn butter is smooth and creamy.

Salt Fish and Potatoes

dry salted cod
potatoes

Tear or cut a medium dry-salted cod into several pieces and soak in cold water overnight. Strain and add enough fresh cold water to cover.

Wash potatoes and remove some of the peel. Add the potatoes to the fish, bring to a boil and cook until potatoes are done.

Serve with hot pork fat and scruncheons or with drawn butter.

Sometimes, in the fall when vegetables were plentiful, boiled turnip and parsnips would be served with the salt fish and potatoes.

In most Newfoundland homes, this is still the most regularly served of all fish dishes.

Fish Hash

fresh or salt codfish
mashed potatoes
onion
salt pork

*Fish hash was made from fresh or salt codfish. Most people
preferred salt fish and often cooked more than enough for a meal
so that there'd be enough left over to make a pot of hash. The hash
was usually served as a supper dish with hot fresh bread buns,
cabbage pickles and rashers.*

To make fish hash remove the skin and bones from left-over boiled fish,
and break the fish into small flakes with a fork. Mash freshly boiled or left-
over potatoes, using three cups of mashed potatoes to 1½ cups of flaked
fish.

Cut one medium onion into small pieces and fry lightly in hot fat. Add
onion to fish and potato mixture and mix well with a wooden spoon.

Fry 3 or 4 slices of salt pork in a deep iron pan. When the rashers are
golden brown, remove them from the pan and put them in a heated oven to
be served with the hash.

Place the hash mixture in the pan with the hot fat and mix thoroughly.
Cover and let steam until the hash is hot.

Cabbage Pickles

This recipe required fresh or pickled cabbage. If pickled cabbage was used, it was necessary to freshen it by soaking in cold water for several days. You would then omit the salt called for in the recipe. Using fresh cabbage, you would need:

> 1 quart chopped white cabbage
> 2 cups chopped onions
> 4 cups vinegar
> ½ cup of white sugar
> 1 tbsp dry mustard
> 2 tbsp pickling spices tied in a muslin bag
> 1 tsp salt
> ½ cup flour

Put cabbage, onions, vinegar and pickling spices in an enamel pot. Boil for ten minutes and remove the bag of spices.

Add sugar and salt.

Mix mustard and flour with enough cold water to make a thin paste. Stir the paste into the vinegar solution and boil slowly for twenty minutes.

Spoon into hot glass jars and seal.

Peas and Melts

herring roe
herring melts
salt pork
flour
onions
potatoes

*Peas and melts are the roe of the female herring and the milt of
the male herring. To make a meal of peas and melts you need
fresh herring landed within a few hours of netting.*

Take a pound of peas and an equal amount of melts. Wash and pat dry.

Fry pork rashers until they are brown and put them in the oven to keep
them hot.

Sprinkle a small amount of flour on the peas and melts and fry them in
the pork fat until they are crisp.

Remove the peas and melts to a hot platter and fry onion rings until
they become limp but not brown.

Boil potatoes and mash them.

Pour the onions over the peas and melts and serve them with a helping
of mashed potatoes and crisp rashers.

Cod Tongues

cod tongues
flour
salt
pepper
pork fat

An iron frying pan is the best utensil to use when cooking fresh cod tongues.

Wash the tongues in slightly salted water to remove the slime and dry them thoroughly with a cup towel.

Mix enough flour to coat the tongues, a little salt, and a dash of pepper in a bowl. Roll the tongues in this mixture until they are thoroughly coated.

Fry out rashers of salt pork until they are crisp and brown.

Pour off some of the hot fat leaving about ½ an inch in the pan.

Fry the tongues in the hot fat over medium heat until they are browned on both sides.

Do not allow the pan to go dry. Pour in more fat when necessary.

When the tongues are crisp and nicely browned, remove them to a hot platter and put them in a heated oven until served.

Stewed Fish and Pastry

cod fish
salt pork
flour
water
potatoes
onions
chives
salt
pepper

Stewed fish may be served with or without the pastry.

Choose a fresh codfish of medium size. To test for freshness, press your fingertips into the skin close to the backbone. If the print of your finger remains, the fish is not as fresh as it should be and therefore will lack some of its flavour.

Scrape off the scales with a sharp knife, working from the tail toward the head. Split the fish and remove the stomach and liver. Remove the head, tail and small fins. Cut out the soundbone and set aside.

Cut the fish into several pieces. Chop the soundbone into sections. Wash both in cold water and drain.

Cut 4 or 5 slices of salt pork into small pieces and fry out to make scruncheons. Remove the scruncheons from the fat and set aside.

Wipe the fish dry and sprinkle with flour. Brown each piece of fish on both sides in the hot fat, using a deep iron frying pan or bake pot.

Add 4 cups of water and 1 teaspoon of salt. Add the soundbone for flavour and remove it later when the meat and sound has fallen from the bone.

Add 4 or 5 potatoes, peeled and sliced, and two coarsely chopped onions. Cook until the potatoes are tender. Add a generous sprinkling of chopped chives and ¼ teaspoon of pepper.

If you are serving the stew without the pastry, serve in soup bowls and sprinkle with scruncheons.

Pastry for Stewed Fish

To make pastry for stewed codfish you will need:

> 1½ cups flour
> 3 level tsps baking powder
> 1 tsp salt
> 1 tbsp fat drippings
> enough cold water to make a medium dough

Put the flour, baking powder and sat together in a bowl and mix them well.

Add the drippings and mix again.

Add the water slowly and mix with your hands.

Press the dough out to a thickness of one inch on a lightly floured board.

When the fish is almost cooked, place the pastry on top of the stew and allow to boil gently for 10 or 12 minutes.

To serve stewed fish and pastry, cut the pastry in triangles and serve it with the stew poured over it.

Cold Dressing for Fresh Fish

This dressing is especially good with cod tongues. You will need:

> 1 cup sugar
> 2 eggs
> 1 tbsp prepared mustard
> a pinch of salt
> 1 cup cream or milk
> ½ cup vinegar

Beat the eggs and add the mustard and sugar slowly. Add the salt, cream and vinegar.

Cook slowly, stirring constantly, until the mixture comes to a boil.

The dressing should be smooth and creamy and cooled before serving.

Fried Cods' Heads

> cods' heads
> salt pork
> flour
> salt
> pepper

Take six medium size fresh cods' heads. Remove the skulls and upper lips. Cut the remaining part of each cod's head into two sections. Cut off the small red sacs (the ears of the fish) from inside the jaws. Scar the skin and remove it from the cheeks. Wash the cods' heads well in cold water.

Cut ½ pound of salt pork into thin rashers and fry them in an iron pan until they are brown. Leave enough fat for frying and reserve the rest.

Dry the cods' heads with a towel and dip them in flour seasoned with salt and pepper

Fry the heads over medium heat and allow each portion to brown before turning them over. If the frying pan goes dry, add more fat, and cook the heads until they are nice and brown on both sides.

When served with boiled potatoes and mashed turnip, six cods' heads will serve three people.

Boiled Salmon

fresh salmon
salt

Remove the gut and liver from a 4 or 5 pound salmon and slosh the salmon clean with sea water. Hold the salmon firmly by the tail and scrape the scales off with a sharp knife.

Place the salmon on a damp cloth and cut off the head and tail. Cut the rest of the fish into cross sections, one piece for each serving. Put the salmon in boiling salted water and boil for 20 minutes or until the fish loses its light pink colour, but be careful not to overcook. Serve with boiled or baked potatoes sprinkled with freshly chopped chives. Garnish with mustard.

Mustard

Mustard was a favourite garnish for all kinds of fresh fish. It was made a few minutes before serving time.

2 tsps dry mustard
4 tsps cold water
a dash pepper

Mix these ingredients together to form a thin paste but mix only as much as you intend to use immediately. Mustard made this way loses its colour and becomes hard when left over for any length of time.

Fried Salmon

fresh salmon
flour
salt
pepper
salt pork

Salmon was usually cleaned in the stage when the catch was landed. Therefore the housewife had very little preparation to do except remove the scales and cut off the head and tail.

Wash the salmon in cold water and wipe it dry with a dish towel. Cut into serving pieces and roll each piece in flour to which a little salt and pepper has been added. Fry rashers of salt pork until they are brown. Remove the rashers and place each piece of floured salmon in the hot fat. Cook until the salmon is lightly browned on each side.

Serve with mashed potatoes and turnip strips. Garnish with mustard or a sprinkling of vinegar.

Salt Herring and Potatoes

6 salt herring
potatoes

Water salt herring until reasonably fresh (3 or 4 days at least). Cut off the heads and tails and put the herring in a boiler of cold water. Bring the water to a boil.

Scrub 6 to 8 potatoes with a vegetable brush and boil them in a separate pot.

Remove the herring from the boiler and drain them. Spread each fish open and remove the backbone by lifting it out gently with the tines of a fork.

Serve with potatoes for a good meal anytime.

Fresh Fried Herring

6 fresh herring
salt pork fat or rashers
flour
salt
pepper

Clean the herring and scrape off the scales. Remove the heads and tails. Wash the herring in cold water and pat dry with a towel.

Put 1 cup of flour in a bowl and mix in 1 teaspoon of salt and ¼ teaspoon of pepper.

Put 2 tablespoons of salt pork fat (or fry out rashers of salt pork) in an iron pan and heat to moderate temperature.

Coat the herring thoroughly with the flour mixture and place them in the pan. (A ten inch pan will hold three herring.) Fry slowly to prevent burning and cook until each side of the herring is a golden brow.

Serve with boiled potatoes. Garnish with mustard or a sprinkling of vinegar.

Fried Brook Trout

trout
salt pork
flour
salt
pepper

Trouting was a favourite pastime for children in St. Leonard's. We fished the Chapel Pond in spring when the ice melted around the shore. Later we waded in the brooks and small gullies where trout fed on the hatching larvae under the muddy banks. A pole, made from a slender birch branch, a ball of string, a few hooks, a bobber, a can of worms, and a little bit of luck was all we needed to catch a meal of trout.

Rinse the trout in slightly salted water to remove the slime. Remove the heads and entrails. Fry pork rashers in an iron frying pan until they are crisp and brown. Sprinkle each trout with flour, salt and pepper. Put the trout in the hot fat and fry them until they are golden brown on both sides. Serve with boiled potatoes and green peas.

Cod Sounds

sounds
potatoes
salt pork
onion

The sound is a strip of membrane lying along the inside of the
backbone of the cod. The portion of backbone to which the sound is
attached is called the soundbone.

In St. Leonard's the sounds were usually salt cured for four or
five months in tubs or wooden boxes. The sounds were simply
removed from the soundbone, scraped clean of clotted blood,
washed, dry salted, and stored until properly cured.

To prepare a meal of sounds, wash the coarse salt from two pounds of
them. Put them to soak in cold water for twenty-four hours, changing the
water once. Strain the water off the sounds and scrape away the black
lining. Put them in a pot of cold water and bring to a boil. Simmer until
cooked. Strain and chop the sounds into bite-size pieces.

Boil three or four potatoes in salted water. Chop coarsely.

Fry out salt pork rashers in an iron pot. When the rashers are fried
crisp, add one chopped onion to the hot fat and stir.

Add the chopped potatoes and sounds. Mix well and serve for breakfast,
dinner, or supper.

Corned Caplin

When the caplin rolled up on the sandy beaches around the end of June, men, women and children lined up with buckets, tubs and pans to fill them with the small silver fish that tumbled knee-deep at the water's edge. The men gathered them in dip nets, wading out to scoop them from the black schools swarming toward the beach.

Caplin were gathered in large quantities for bait and fertilizer and also for food. They were preserved for winter food by salting in brine for a day or so, then spread to dry in the sun until they were cured enough to last through the winter.

Dried caplin were roasted on live coals or cooked on flat pans in the oven, and were often used as snacks between meals or for late night lunches.

Fried Fresh Caplin

3 dozen fresh caplin
pork rashers
salt
pepper

Caplin are such small fish they require very little preparation to cook. Remove the head and the small intestine will slip from the split caplin. When the caplin are cleaned, wash them in cold water and pat them dry.

Fry out pork rashers until they are crisp. Remove the rashers from the pan and keep them hot in the oven.

Mix 1 cup of flour with 1 teaspoon of salt and ¼ teaspoon of pepper. Dredge each caplin in the flour mixture and fry in the hot fat until golden brown. Serve for breakfast, dinner or supper with bread and butter and a cup of hot tea.

Boiled Rounders

rounders
potatoes
turnip
parsnip
drawn butter

Rounders were small codfish. They were heavily dry-salted for winter keeping, and since the soundbone was not removed, the fish retained its round shape. Hence the name "rounders."

To cook three or four rounders, soak the fish in cold water for three or four days, changing the water several times. When the rounders are fresh enough to cook, wash them well and cut off the tails. Put them in a pot of cold water and simmer for an hour.

While the rounders are cooking, scrub 5 medium potatoes, peel and slice a small turnip, peel 3 parsnips, and cook these vegetables in boiling salted water.

When the fish and vegetables are cooked, remove the skin and bones from the fish and arrange on a dinner plate with a serving of each vegetable and a few spoonfuls of drawn butter.

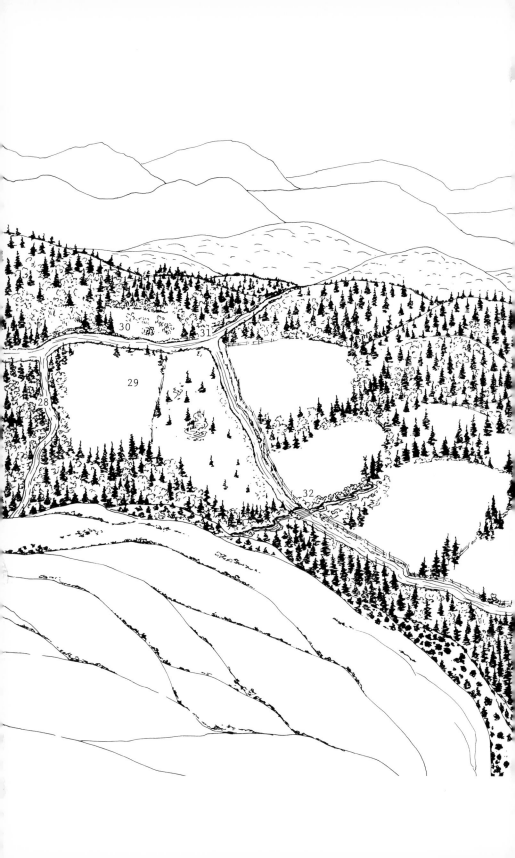

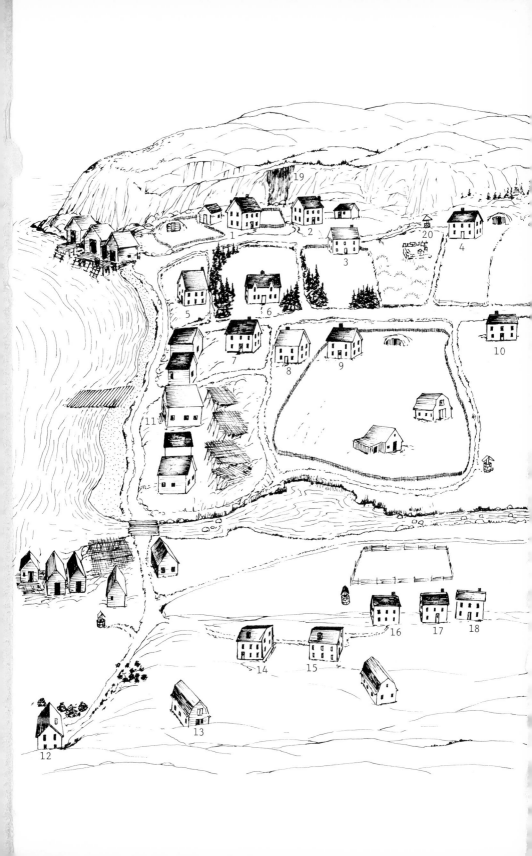

St. Leonard's Around 1925

Legend

1 — Ned Leonard's
2 — Mr. Igg's
3 — Tom Leonard's
4 — Jim Leonard's
5 — John Joe's
6 — Pat Sullivan's
7 — Ned Rodgers'
8 — Phonse Leonard's
9 — John Collins'
10 — Jerry Callahan's
11 — Jim Leonard's Store (*Agent for W.W. Wareham*)
12 — Henry Rodgers'
13 — Mrs. El's
14 — Mrs. Fred's
15 — Jim Rodgers'
16 — Annie F. Sullivan's
17 — Tom Sullivan's
18 — Jim Sullivan's
19 — The Scrape
20 — The Spring Well
21 — Liza's Rock
22 — The Salmon Hole
23 — Chapel Pond
24 — Ladore
25 — Calvary Hill
26 — The Old Church
27 — Father Walsh's Well
28 — The Graveyard Road
29 — The Pond Field
30 — The Orchard
31 — Mrs. Dunn's
32 — The Fairy Dell
33 — St. Peter's School
34 — The Green Gates
35 — The Church of the Assumption
36 — The Priest's House

Meat and Vegetables and the Like

Cabbage Hash

Hash was served as a supper dish. It was usually made from leftover fish or meat mixed with vegetables.

During the years of the Depression, hash was made from vegetables only. Cabbage hash was a favourite meal on cold winter evenings when the chores were done and families gathered in big comfortable kitchens with the lamps lit and the Waterloo stove sending waves of heat into every corner.

When the cabbage bins in the root cellars were empty, pickled cabbage was used and it made an equally appetizing meal.

cabbage
left-over vegetables
onion
salt pork fat
pepper

Chop the cabbage and other left-over vegetables from a salt beef dinner into bite-size pieces. Peel 1 onion and chop finely.

Cook the onion in a frying pan until transparent, with ¼ cup of hot pork fat.

Tumble the vegetables into the pan and stir. Toss lightly over a hot damper until the vegetables are thoroughly heated.

Some cooks preferred to mash the ingredients with a potato masher, then heat the hash in a pot in which rashers had been fried.

In either case, season the hash with pepper and serve it piping hot.

Pickled Cabbage

cabbage
brine
salt—peter

Remove the stump and withered leaves. Check each head of cabbage for slugs and foreign matter. Cut each head into quarters and wash well in cold water. Pack the cabbage in beef barrels with a mixture of brine and salt peter.

Some people preferred to use the left-over brine from salt beef or pork. Others made their own formula from a mixture of coarse salt and water, adding salt—peter in the process of packing.

The strength of the brine was an important factor. If there was any doubt about this, they took a potato and dropped it into the barrel of brine to test it. If the potato floated to the top, then the mixture was salt enough to preserve the cabbage for long periods of time.

Then the cabbage was packed in layers and heavy weights placed over it. The weights were used to keep the cabbage below the surface so that it would be properly cured.

The pickling process takes about three months.

To prepare the cabbage for a meal, wash it well in cold water to remove the salt-peter. Place it in tubs of cold water to freshen and change the water frequently. When the cabbage is fresh enough to use in cooking, use as in Salt Beef and Cabbage.

Salt Beef and Cabbage

3 or 4 lbs of salt beef
1 turnip
1 head of cabbage
3 or 4 carrots
3 or 4 parsnips
6 to 8 potatoes

Soak salt beef in cold water overnight.

To cook the beef, strain it and put it in a deep boiler. Cover with cold water and boil over medium heat until the meat can be pierced with a fork. Prepare the vegetables beforehand or while the beef is cooking.

Remove the faded leaves from the cabbage, cut into quarters and remove the core.

Scrape the carrots and if they are large, cut them into lengths. Peel the turnip and cut it into 1 inch slices. Peel parsnips and cut in halves. Peel potatoes and cut the large ones in halves. Wash all vegetables in cold water. Add the vegetables to the boiling beef liquid and cook until done , but be careful not to overcook them.

This meal was often referred to as Thursday Dinner. If it was served on Sundays or special occasions, peas pudding or figgy duff or both were added to give it a festive touch.

Cabbage Soup

½ pound salt beef (cut in cubes)
1 small or ½ a large head of cabbage
1 onion
½ medium turnip
3 or 4 carrots
4 or 5 potatoes
flour, salt and pepper

Wash salt beef in cold water and drain. Wash cabbage, separate leaves and remove core. Chop in medium pieces. Scrape carrots and cut in 1 inch chunks. Peel turnip and chop in thick wedges. Cut onion in quarters.

Place beef in a boiler. Add 5 cups cold water and boil until beef is tender but firm. Add vegetables and cook until tender. Add a dash of pepper and taste for salt seasoning. If stock has diminished, add hot water to equal the original amount.

Make a thickening of flour and water. Make sure the mixture is smooth and free from lumps of dry flour. Add to boiling soup slowly, stirring with a wooden spoon. When the soup has the texture of a light gravy, it's time to serve.

If salt beef were not available, fat back pork or left-over stock from salt beef and cabbage dinner was substituted, the latter, containing lots of nutrition, was referred to as "pot likker."

Rabbit Stew

1 or 2 rabbits
1 turnip
1 onion
4 to 6 potatoes
salt pork
pepper and salt

Rabbits should be hung at least 24 hours before cooking.

To skin a rabbit, lay it on a flat surface covered with paper. Cut circular lines around the hind legs just above the paws. Pull the skin away from the quarters, making sure the fur is turned outwards. Keep pulling with a steady motion until the complete skin is removed as far as the neck. Pull out the forelegs and remove the paws. Cut the skin away from the head and pull all the way. Remove the hind paws from the carcass and wipe the meat with a damp cloth to remove any hairs that may have stuck to the meat.

Slit the paunch and remove the entrails. Make sure the gall bladder is removed from the liver. Save the liver and heart for the stew.

If you cook more than one rabbit to make a stew, reserve the heads and baskets (rib cage) for soup.

Fry 2 or 3 rashers of salt pork in an iron pot until crisp. Cut the rabbit into sections as follows: 2 hind quarters, 2 forelegs, the back including the kidneys, the basket and head. Brown the rabbit in hot fat. Add the liver and heart. Do not remove the pork rashers. Cover and let steam on low heat for about 10 minutes. Add enough hot water to cover the rabbit meat. Boil gently until the rabbit is almost cooked.

Peel the turnip and cut it into chunks. Peel the onion and cut in slices. Add these vegetables to the meat and boil until tender. Add pepper and salt to taste. Boil the potatoes in their jackets in a separate pot with a little salt.

If the liquid in the rabbit pot has evaporated, add more water to make the gravy. Thicken with a mixture of flour and cold water.

The rabbit meat should be tender but not separated from the bones, and the turnip should be firm.

Serve on heated plates with the boiled potatoes.

If a pastry is preferred with the stew, place it over the rabbit portions and bake in a hot oven before adding the extra liquid to make the gravy.

Baked Rabbit

1 rabbit
ingredients for dressing (below)
salt pork rashers
flour
water
salt

Prepare rabbit as for rabbit stew but do not cut in pieces. Prepare the dressing as follows:

2 cups grated breadcrumbs
1 tsp salt
1 or 2 small onions (cut fine)
2 tbsps savory
1 tbsp butter

Mix all the ingredients together in a bowl. Stuff the dressing into the basket (rib cage) and secure with clean parcel twine or white thread. Dust a little flour on the bottom of a baking pan. Lay the rabbit on the pan and put 2 or 3 salt pork rashers on top. Bake covered for 2 hours or until the meat is tender.

Remove the cover and allow the meat to brown. Add hot water to make juice. Make a plain pastry and lay it over the rabbit. When the pastry is done and slightly browned, remove it to a hot platter. Thicken the juice with a thin paste of flour and cold water. Add salt to taste.

Serve with boiled potatoes, carrot and mashed turnip.

Deer In a Pot

  deer meat
  salt pork rashers
  flour
  water
  salt

Fry out a couple of pork rashers in an iron pot until brown. Take any cut of meat from deer that has been dressed and prepared for food. Roll in a little flour and brown on each side.

Add 1 cup of water and cook slowly until the meat is done. Add salt to taste. Add enough water to the pot to make a generous amount of gravy. Thicken with a mixture of flour and water.

Carve the meat and serve with slices of homemade bread smothered in gravy.

Meat Soup

A pot of soup was for "eating and drinking." It was made from fresh beef, wild ducks, chicken, rabbit or beef bones. No matter what the source, the soup was intended as a meal. Dumplings were served with all soups and now and then other vegetables such as potatoes were served as a special addition. The same ingredients were used for all meat soups.

meat	rice or barley
carrot	salt and pepper
turnip	flour
onion	water
parsnip	

Simmer the meat until it falls from the bone. Remove the bones from the liquid and add more water to allow enough soup for the number to be served.

Add diced carrot, turnip cut in chunks, onion, parsnip, rice or barley. Cook until the vegetables are tender.

Season to taste. Boil dumplings in the liquid, then thicken with a little flour and cold water paste after the dumplings have been removed from the boiler.

Serve in bowls with the meat and potatoes on a separate plate. If there happens to be dumplings left over, use them as a dessert with jam or molasses sauce.

In the Depression days or when fresh meat was scarce, soup was made from watered salt beef, vegetable water or "pot likker."

Venison Stew

The shoulder, neck and rib sections of caribou or moose were used for making stews.

venison
pork rashers
flour
water
carrots
turnip
onion
potatoes

Chop the meat and bones into pieces.

Fry out a couple of pork rashers in an iron pot. Dredge the meat with flour and brown on all sides in the hot fat. Add water and simmer for an hour or so until the meat is tender.

Add chunks of carrot, turnip and onion. Cook slowly and salt to taste. Boil potatoes in salted water, leaving the skin on.

Make a thin gravy by thickening the stew liquid with a mixture of flour and cold water.

Baking powder pastry may be cooked on the stew before adding the thickening.

Dandelion Dinner

Dandelion is an early spring green. Its leaves are rich in iron, the roots are edible and the posies produce a fine wine.

dandelion
salt beef
carrot
turnip
potatoes

Soak salt beef in cold water overnight as for cabbage dinners. Wash and carefully pick over the dandelion leaves.

Prepare the carrot and turnip. Add to the beef liquid and cook until tender. Remove from the pot and put in the dandelion. Cook for 15 minutes. Boil potatoes separately.

Dandelion can be eaten all summer but as the season progresses the flavour will become stronger and have a bitter taste. To offset this, put the leaves in cold water and bring to a boil, then put them in the salt beef liquid and simmer until tender.

Salt Pork Gravy

¼ lb salt pork
4 tbsp flour
3 cups hot water
1 onion (cut fine)
salt and pepper
flour
water

Wash the pork in warm water and cut into small cubes. Cook the pork cubes in a frying pan until crisp and brown. Remove to a hot dish and keep hot.

Toss the onion in the hot fat. Add hot water slowly and stir the brownings from the bottom and sides of the pan. Let simmer.

Mix flour and cold water to a thin paste, add to the hot fat mixture to make a golden brown gravy. Add a dash of pepper and taste before salting.

Add the pork cubes just before serving.

Head Cheese

1 cow's head
½ cup onion (minced)
2 tsps savory
salt and pepper

Take all the skin from the cow's head and chop into pieces. Remove all the useless parts, i.e., nostrils, ear parts, lips, teeth, eyes, palate and any remaining sections of the windpipe.

Soak in cold water overnight. Strain off the water and rinse several times to remove signs of blood.

Place in a large pot, cover with cold water, add a little salt and simmer until the meat falls from the bones.

Cool. Remove all the bones and chop or grind the meat very fine. Put the chopped meat back into the pot, add a little more water. Add the onion and savory. Add the pepper and salt to taste.

Simmer for ½ an hour. Pour into small earthen jars. Seal the jars and put them in the cellar or some other cool place to set.

Roast Leg of Goat

Goats were kept mainly to supply milk and butter. Goat's milk was considered less susceptible to harmful bacteria than cow's milk and was highly recommended for babies and young children by local mid-wives. Occasionally a goat would be slaughtered for meat.

leg of goat
vinegar
mint leaves
onion
flour
water

Remove the thin membrane from all parts of the meat. Rub the meat with a mixture of vinegar and crushed mint leaves.

Place on a rack in an iron roasting pan and bake in a moderate oven until tender and slightly browned.

Remove to a hot platter and strain the excess fat from the bottom of the roasting pan. Add 1 onion, cut in small pieces. Brown the onion in the hot drippings and add 3 cups of hot water. Let boil for 10 minutes and thicken with a mixture of flour and cold water. Serve the meat with boiled potato, mashed turnip and buttered carrot.

Shoulder roast of goat was cooked in the same manner and the rib section was used for stews.

Blood Pudding

Cattle, sheep and pigs were usually killed in late fall or early winter. This time of year was chosen for two reasons; the animals were in prime condition from feeding on the lush "after grass" and late clover growth in the local pastures and there would be less chance of meat spoilage because of the cold frosty weather.

The blood is obtained by piercing the jugular vein as quickly as possible after the beast is killed. To an estimated quart of blood, add a slight handful of coarse salt. This should be done while the blood is still warm.

allow ½ cup fine breadcrumbs to 1 cup salted blood

Add to this mixture the following ingredients:

> **1 cup chopped suet**
> **2 large onions (cut fine)**
> **½ tsp pepper**
> **½ tsp allspice**

Put the suet, onions, pepper and allspice into a bowl and mix thoroughly. Pour breadcrumbs and blood mixture into the bowl and stir with a wooden spoon until ingredients are well combined. Set aside.

Place the small intestines to soak in vats containing cold water. Cut in convenient lengths and turn inside out. Wash each section until perfectly clean. Rinse several times and drain them on wooden trays.

Tie one end of the intestine section securely and spoon the mixture in until three quarters full. Tie the opening and repeat until the pudding mixture is used up. Immerse in cold water in large boilers and bring to a boil. Allow to boil slowly until the filling has expanded and the sacs are firm. Remove from the boiling water and let drain. Hang in a cool place and allow to set.

Blood puddings were served for breakfast as a treat. Slice the pudding and fry lightly in pork fat. Serve with slices of hot buttered toast or serve with fried potatoes and cabbage pickle for an enjoyable supper dish.

Round Pea Soup

Green or yellow round peas may be used for this recipe.

1 lb round peas (soak overnight in cold water)
1½ lb salt beef (watered 3 or 4 hours and drained)
2 medium carrots
1 small turnip
1 onion
1 parsnip

Add the pieces of salt beef to the peas, using the water in which the peas have been soaked. Add more water if necessary. Boil gently until the beef is tender and the peas still retain their shape.

Prepare the carrots, turnip and parsnips. Cut them into cubes and add to the liquid. Simmer until the vegetables are tender.

Remove the beef to a warm platter. Add sliced onion to the soup and simmer until the onion is limp.

In a separate pot, cook 4 or 5 potatoes in their jackets. If the soup is thin, make a thickening from flour and cold water and stir in until the desired consistency is reached.

Serve the soup in warm bowls. Slice the beef and serve with the potatoes on the side.

To serve round green peas with meat and gravy dinner, soak the peas overnight and add a pinch of salt to the water in which they are boiled. Be very careful not to let them boil dry. When the peas are cooked, add a pinch of pepper and a dab of butter. Stir lightly and serve.

Scot's Tripe

Tripe is the stomach tissue of cud-chewing animals. After thorough cleansing, the tripe was packed in dry salt and in some cases pickled.

In the spring of the year when fresh meat was scarce, several varieties of meals were made with tripe as a base.

One such recipe was called "Scot's Tripe."

The tripe was taken from the dry salt or pickle and watered for a couple of days. Then it was boiled slowly for an hour or so to make a meal of Scot's Tripe you need:

> **boiled tripe**
> **salt pork rashers**
> **water**
> **turnip**
> **potatoes**
> **onion**
> **salt and pepper**

Cut the boiled tripe into bite size pieces. Fry pork rashers until brown. Add the chopped tripe and let fry for a few minutes.

Add hot water, allowing 2 cups of water to 2 cups of chopped tripe.

Add 2 cups of chopped turnip, 2 cups of chopped potato and 1 small onion. Add pepper and salt to taste. Boil until vegetables are tender.

Serve with a helping of pickled cabbage, soda bread and a glass of spruce beer.

Baked Turr

turrs
bread crumbs
butter
onions
salt
pepper
savory
salt pork
water

Grandfather was always pleased when there were a lot of turrs to be picked. Too old to go "bird huntin'," he enjoyed picking them, especially if there was an audience of youngsters to inject complimentary remarks about how fast and how well he could do it.

"I allow you've picked hundreds of turrs and sea ducks in your day, eh skipper?"

"Yes m'son, I have," he would say, glad of the opportunity to yarn about those other years when he slung his long-tom on his shoulders, ran to where his punt was hauled up and rowed in the grey mist of early morning to "just off the Red Land" and how he waited, sometimes for twenty minutes with his finger on the trigger, ready to fire as the turrs broke water or, on occasion, to shoot them on the wing.

Grandfather would time himself to impress his audience. "If a man can't pick a turr clean in twenty minutes, there's something wrong," he would say.

A sailcloth apron was spread over the knees and the turr balanced breast-up with the head hanging downwards. The feathers were plucked by the pressure of the thumb and forefinger pulling the feathers away from the skin with a jerking motion. The turr was turned around until all the feathers were removed. When the picking was finished, the feathers were saved to make feather beds and pillows.

A good picker like my grandfather, would remove most of the down in the process, but generally a red hot iron rod or an old rasp was applied and the fat scraped off with a sharp knife. The head, wings and webs were cut off and the stomach and liver removed. Then the turrs were washed in cold water containing a little baking soda and left to drain.

Stuff each turr with dressing (bread crumbs, butter, onions, salt, pepper and savory).

Fry out a couple pork rashers until crisp. Brown each turr in the hot fat. Drain off the excess fat and put the turrs in a bake pot in a moderate oven. Bake for 1 hour then cover and continue to bake until the meat is tender.

Place the turrs on a hot platter and leave in a fairly warm oven. Put the bake pot on the hot damper and add enough water to make gravy.

While the turr is baking, prepare potatoes, turnip and carrots. Cook in boiling salted water.

Thicken the gravy with a paste of cold water and flour. Season with salt.

Serve ½ a turr with a portion of each vegetable. Cover with hot gravy. If a pastry is used with this meal, it must be baked by placing it over the turrs in the bake pot before making the gravy.

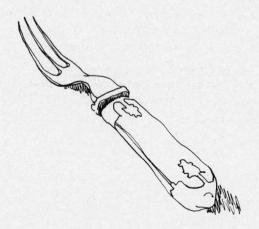

Liver and Lights

1 to 2 lbs beef liver
1 lb lights (the lungs)
3 or 4 rashers of salt pork
4 medium potatoes
1 small turnip
1 onion
2 or 3 carrots
pepper and salt to taste

Fry pork rashers in iron pan until brown. Cut liver and lights into bite size pieces. Dust with flour and brown lightly in the pork fat. Add one cup of warm water and let simmer until liver is tender.

Peel potatoes, turnip and onion. Scrape carrot and wash in cold water. Cut vegetables into chunks and add to liver mixture. Cook until vegetables are tender but do not overcook. Add the pepper and salt.

Thicken liquid with a thin paste of flour and cold water.

Peas Pudding

Mix the following ingredients and put the mixture into a pudding bag that has been dipped in cold water.

1 lb yellow split peas
¼ tsp salt
small piece fat pork

Gather the bag loosely at the top to allow room for the peas to swell. Tie securely and soak the bag containing the peas, in cold water overnight. Place in the dinner boiler and cook for 1 hour.

Before turning the pudding out of the bag, press with wooden spoon. Allow to set for about 10 minutes. Turn out on a hot platter. The peas pudding should hold its shape and the texture be such that it can be sliced for servings.

Fried Whale

3 or 4 whale steaks ½ inch thick
3 or 4 rashers salt pork
2 medium onions
salt and pepper

Arctic steak was the fancy name given to the flesh of the young whale. The meat was obtained from the whaling station at Rose-au-rue. It wasn't sold, mind you, but was available to anyone who had a mind to sample it.

The method of curing whale to keep it preserved for a short while was simple but effective. The meat was cut in large chunks and hung in the sun. This process was called "weathering". The heat of the sun penetrated the meat to a depth of one inch forming a dark hard crust.

To prepare the meat for cooking, the parched section was removed and the inside meat would be found fresh and very cold. The only way to preserve it for any length of time was by salting, but salt whale was never a very popular dish.

Use grease from fried pork rashers. Place steaks on a hot iron pan. Fry quickly, turning only once. Use pepper and salt moderately while frying. Remove to hot platter and add chopped onion to juice in the frying pan. Brown slightly and add hot water if necessary. Add a little salt to season. Serve the steaks with the juice and onions poured over them.

Stewed Beans and Pastry

1 lb dried Navy beans
fat back pork
carrot
turnip
onion
salt and pepper

Wash the Navy beans and soak in 3 cups of cold water overnight. To prepare as a meal, put the beans in a heavy skillet. Add enough cold water to cover the beans.

Add ½ a pound of fat back pork cut in cubes. Boil until the beans are tender.

Add enough hot water when necessary to cover the beans. They burn easily in the process of stewing and must have an adequate amount of liquid to prevent this from happening.

Add ½ cup of cubed carrot, ½ cup of cubed turnip, 1 small onion (chopped) and salt and pepper to taste. Simmer until the vegetables are tender.

To make the pastry you need:

3 cups flour
3 tsps baking powder
2 tsps salt
1 tbsp butter

Rub the butter into the flour. Add the salt and baking powder. Mix with cold water until the dough is medium soft. Roll to ½ inch thickness on a floured board.

Lay the pastry over the beans and vegetables and simmer until light and flaky. Cut the pastry into serving portions, place on heated plates, and cover with generous helpings of stewed beans.

Baked Beans

1 lb dried Navy beans
½ lb fat back pork (cut in thick slices)
3 tbsp molasses
1 tsp dry mustard
1 tsp salt
dash pepper

Wash beans in cold water and strain. Place in an iron bake pot. Add enough cold water to cover. Stir in molasses and mustard. Add the salt and pepper and stir thoroughly.

Cover the pot and bake in a hot oven for 3 or 4 hours. Add more water to cover ingredients as water evaporates. Stir occasionally. When cooked the beans should be deep brown in colour and firm in texture.

Serve with brown bread or hot toutens.

Split Pea Soup

1 lb split peas (green or yellow)
1 lb salt beef
1 cup cubed turnip
1 cup finely chopped carrot
1 tbsp sugar
pepper
1 onion

Although the ingredients for making green pea soup were the same as for yellow pea soup, the latter was usually favoured.

Soak the salt beef in cold water overnight, or if the soup was intended for a supper meal, 2 or 3 hours of soaking would be enough if the meat was washed well in cold water beforehand.

Wash the peas in cold water and strain.

Cut the watered beef in small pieces and put in a boiler with the peas. Add a quart of cold water. Bring to a boil and let simmer until the peas are almost done.

Prepare the turnip and carrot and cut into small cubes. Add to the hot liquid.

Peel the onion, cut fine and add. When the vegetables are done, stir in the sugar and a dash of pepper. Stir gently and remove to the back damper until time to serve.

Dumplings for Pea Soup

2 cups flour
1 tsp salt
4 level tsps baking powder
1 tbsp beef fat
cold water

When cooking dumplings with the pea soup, omit the sugar and pepper from the soup until the dumplings are finished cooking. Place the dumplings in a hot dish and put them in the oven to keep warm. Add the sugar and pepper as before.

Measure the flour and salt into a bowl. Rub the beef fat into the flour mixture. Add the baking powder and mix through the flour with the fingertips. Add the cold water, a small portion at a time. Mix with the hands until the dough is firm.

Break off equal portions and form into balls. Drop into boiling soup and cook for 6 to 8 minutes, according to the size.

If the dough becomes sticky, use a little flour or fat on the hands to form the dumplings.

Stuffed Beef Heart

beef heart
dressing ingredients (below)
salt pork fat
carrots
turnip
potatoes
flour
water

Soak the heart in cold water to remove all traces of blood. Trim and clean the tubes.

Make a dressing of grated bread, onions, savory, salt and pepper.

Fill the tubes with the dressing and tie firmly by winding string around the heart. If all the dressing is not used, put the remainder in a small pan, add a spoonful of butter, mix and cover. Bake for 20 minutes.

Put the heart in a bake pot with 2 tablespoons of pork fat. Put the bake pot on top of the stove and brown the heart by turning several times.

Add 1 cup of water, cover and place in the oven. Bake 2 hours or until tender.

Dice 2 carrots. Cut 1 small turnip in small pieces. Peel 4 medium potatoes and cut in halves.

Put the vegetables in the pot with the heart. Cover and bake for 20 minutes.

Remove the heart and potatoes to a hot dish and season the liquid and thicken with a mixture of flour and water.

Slice the heart and serve with the potatoes and vegetable gravy.

Lamb Stew

2 lbs lamb breast, neck or shoulder
2 tbsps flour
2 tbsps salt pork fat
6 potatoes
6 small carrots
1 onion
1 cup chopped turnip
flour
salt and pepper

Dredge the meat with flour and brown well in the hot fat. Season with salt and pepper, cover with water and simmer until almost cooked. Add the onion and other vegetables and cook 30 minutes longer. Mix flour and water to a smooth paste and add to the liquid to make a thin gravy.

Serve with dumplings.

Shepherd's Pie

Use left-over lamb stew. Line a bake pot with hot mashed potatoes. Fill the centre with hot stew, cover with a layer of mashed potatoes and bake in a hot oven for 15 minutes or until the potatoes are browned.

Fried Kidney

beef kidney
flour
salt pork fat
salt and pepper

Wash the kidneys and remove the skin. Cover with cold water and bring to a boil. Put the pot on the back damper and simmer for ten minutes. Cool.

Cut out the cords and then remove all the fat tissue. Slice thin, dip each piece in flour, and fry in the hot fat until brown. Remove the kidneys from the pan, add flour to the fat, stirring well until thoroughly brown. Add boiling water and stir until smooth. Return the kidneys to the pan, add pepper and salt. Cover and simmer for 1 hour, adding more water when needed.

Fresh Butter

Fresh butter was made by churning the cream. The term 'fresh' was applied only because it had not been bought in a shop. The butter contained salt for seasoning and was often packed in empty butter tubs for the winter. Scalded cream produced a better product in taste and colour than the unscalded. The unscalded, or sweet cream as it was called, was much better for whipping or using in tea.

Method for scalding cream:

Put the milk in large enamel basins and let it set for 24 hours. Put the basins over pots of boiling water and steam until the cream becomes thick and wrinkled.

Remove the basins of milk to a cool place and leave them for a day or so. The scalded cream is then skimmed from the milk and stored in crocks until there is enough to make fresh butter.

Method for making fresh butter:

Put the scalded cream into wooden churns. Keep the beaters in motion by hand until the butter forms. Strain off the buttermilk and rinse the butter several times in cold water. Mix salt in with a wooden spatula. The amount of salt can vary and should be used with discretion.

The butter was then made into separate lots called 'prints'.

Butter prints were made of wood, in different sizes and designs. They were dipped in cold water and the butter was pressed into the shape, smoothed off with a damp spatula and tapped gently until it came out.

The prints of butter were placed on rhubarb leaves to harden, packed in earthen jars and stored in a cool place.

Spruce Beer

*Spruce Beer was made from ground spruce boughs. Ground spruce
has nothing to do with spruce trees. It grows in turfy ground on the
dry barrens and looks like a shrub.*

Pick an armload of the spruce with as little of the stumpy part as possible.
Place in an iron kettle and press down firmly. Fill the kettle with cold water
and steep for a couple of hours.

Strain liquid into a small keg or wooden tub. Add the same amount of
water to the spruce and steep again. Strain and add to the first amount of
liquid. Let cool to lukewarm.

To approximately 3 gallons of liquid add 1 1/2 yeast cake and 3 1/2 cups of
white sugar. Slice 1 medium potato and add to the contents. Let stand in
open brew for a week.

Stir the brew once a day. When the froth has worked off, strain and
bottle.

*Empty rum bottles were ideal containers and anyone could make
corks from net floats.*

*A caution: make sure the open brew is in a warm place. Cold
temperatures will kill the power of the yeast.*

*Add a few pins of spruce to each bottle and set aside in a cool
cellar or the back porch for a couple of weeks.*

*Don't shake the bottle and hold your breath when you pop the
cork.*

*This was a favourite brew for a Garden Party and you could
buy 2 glasses of it for 5 cents.*

Call Cannon

*The first meal of Call Cannon for the year was cooked on the evening
of the thirty-first of October. By that time most of the vegetables were
harvested and put in the root cellars for winter keeping.*

*On this occasion, neighbours would share and exchange the
various vegetables from their gardens with each other, and the night
of the meal was always called Call Cannon Night.*

    1 medium head cabbage
    3 carrots
    1 medium turnip
    6 to 8 potatoes
    ¼ cup butter
    salt and pepper

Peel potatoes and turnip and scrape the carrots. Remove faded leaves from
the cabbage and wash the vegetables in cold water. Drain them well. Chop
the cabbage coarsely and cut the potatoes, turnip and carrots into fairly
small pieces.

Heat water to boiling point in a heavy skillet. Add 1 teaspoon of salt.
Add the vegetables and cook until tender.

Strain the cooked vegetables through a colander and mash them well.
Pour the water from the skillet. Return the mashed vegetables to the
skillet and add the butter and pepper and salt to taste.

Stir the mixture with a wooden spoon, let it get piping hot and serve.

Breads, Cookies, Cakes and Such

Barm

Long before Royal Yeast became available in the shops in St. Leonard's, the housewives cultivated their own yeast in the form of hop vines. Hops grew in many kitchen gardens. The vines required very little attention. They clung to fences and walls, climbed around old trees, and were picked before fullblown.

At the picking stage, the blooms were called hop buds. They were gathered in large quantities and hung in bags to dry.

To make barm you need:

> **hop buds**
> **water**
> **sugar**
> **flour**

Steep 2 cups of hop buds in 4 cups of water. Strain and let liquid cool to lukewarm. Add 1 tablespoon of sugar and mix in flour to make a medium soft dough. Cover and let rise in a warm place.

Homemade Yeast

> **2 oz dried hops**
> **4 qts water**
> **½ cup salt**
> **6 medium potatoes**
> **1 qt flour**
> **½ cup brown sugar**

Boil the hops in water for ½ an hour. Strain and cool to lukewarm. Place the flour, salt and brown sugar in an earthen bowl. Pour in half the liquid and stir well. Add the remainder of the liquid and mix thoroughly. Let stand for three days. On the third day, add the potatoes, boiled and mashed fine. Let stand one more day, then store in covered jars.

Depression Bread

Housewives were disappointed in the result of their first efforts to produce a delectable rising of bread from the flour issued on Government Relief orders during the Depression of the 1930s.

Husbands complained, children complained and the housewives complained most of all. In essence, the flour was a mixture of brown flour, wheat germ, rolled oats, rye and other healthful ingredients, but it was not what they were used to and it took a while before they finally came up with a recipe that produced a reasonably palatable batch of bread.

5 cups Dole flour
5 cups white flour
½ cup molasses
1 yeast cake
2 tbsp fat
1 tbsp salt
1 cup warm water to soak the yeast
4 cups warm water
1 tsp sugar

Add 1 teaspoon of sugar to 1 cup of warm water. Add the yeast cake and soak until soft. Add enough white flour to make a soft dough. Cover and let rise.

Mix both kinds of flour together in a bread pan. Add the salt. Rub in the fat with the fingertip. Add the molasses to 2 cups of warm water and stir into the flour mixture. Add the yeast dough and enough warm water to make a stiff bread dough. Turn out on a floured board and knead well. Put it back in the bread pan, cover and set in a warm place to rise overnight.

Next morning knead down and let rise again. Form the dough into loaves, put into greased baking pans, cover and let rise again for 1 hour.

Bake in a moderate oven until done.

Blueberry Cake

1½ cups flour
1 cup sugar
2 eggs
¼ cup margarine
½ cup milk
2 tsps baking powder
½ tsp salt
1 cup blueberries

Cream margarine thoroughly. Add sugar gradually. Cream together well. Add beaten eggs. Sift flour, baking powder and salt together three times. Add the flour mixture and milk to the egg batter. Mix well. Fold in berries. Pour into a greased loaf pan and bake in oven 350 degrees for about 40 minutes.

Sprinkle top with boiled icing while hot and let the cake cool thoroughly before serving.

Fresh Bread Buns

Break off equal portions of bread dough that has been rising overnight. Use a little flour to form each portion into a bun. Place close together on a greased baking pan and let rise for ten or fifteen minutes. Bake in a hot oven for 20 to 25 minutes. Brush with butter and serve while hot.

Soda Bread

3 cups flour
¼ cup sugar
1 tsp salt
1½ tsps soda
½ cup lard
1 egg
1-1/3 cups sour milk

Sift flour, sugar, salt and soda together. Mix the lard into the flour mixture with the tips of the fingers until it feels like coarse meal.

Add the egg (well beaten) together with the sour milk.

Turn the dough out on a floured board. Use a little flour to keep the dough off your fingers. Knead lightly and shape into a circular loaf. Scar the dough with a sharp knife and bake in an iron bake pot for one hour in a hot oven.

Toutens

bread dough
salt pork

Toutens make a tasty breakfast or supper dessert at any time but one must have a rising of bread on the go in order to make them.

When the bread has been kneaded and ready to bake, cut off small portions of the dough and flatten between the palms of the hands using a little flour. Try to have each portion about the same size.

Fry salt pork rashers until crisp and brown. Take up the rashers and put in a warm oven.

Place the toutens in the hot fat and watch the dough rise quickly. Keep turning in the hot fat until the sides are nicely browned and the dough is cooked through.

Serve with molasses sauce or jam and crisp rashers on the side.

Figgy Duff

2 cups bread crumbs or 2 cups flour
1 cup raisins
½ cup molasses
¼ melted butter
1 tsp baking soda
1 tsp each allspice and cinnamon
½ tsp ground ginger
1 tbsp hot water
¼ tbsp salt
½ cup flour (only if you are using the bread crumbs)

Soak stale bread and crusts in cold water for a few minutes. Squeeze out the water and combine with raisins, molasses, salt and spices. Mix with a fork.

Add the melted butter and the soda which has been dissolved in the hot water. Add the flour and mix well.

Spoon the dough into a pudding bag and boil for 1½ hours.

If you use flour instead of bread crumbs, proceed in the same manner but omit the extra ½ cup of flour.

Sour Milk Buns

2 cups flour
1 cup sour milk
1½ tsps baking soda
1 tsp salt
½ cup rendered fat or lard

Put the flour in a bowl. Rub in the fat and add the salt. Add the soda to the sour milk and stir until it foams. Pour this liquid into the flour mixture and mix lightly until the flour is evenly dampened.

Knead the dough into a greased bun pan and scar in squares with a sharp knife.

Bake in a moderate oven until nicely browned. Turn out on a clean cloth and break off each square while hot.

Cocoa Cake

1¾ cups flour
½ cup cocoa
1¼ cups sugar
½ tsp salt
1 tsp soda
1 tsp baking powder
¼ cup butter or rendered fat
1 egg
1¼ cups sour milk

Sift together flour, cocoa, sugar, salt, soda and baking powder. Rub in the butter or fat with the fingertips. Beat the egg and add to the milk.

Mix the egg and milk into the flour mixture with a wooden spoon until all the ingredients are well blended.

Bake in a moderate oven for ¾ of an hour or until a steel knitting needle comes out dry when inserted in the centre of the cake.

Fresh milk can be made sour by adding a spoonful of vinegar.

Rice Pudding

1 cup water
1 cup rice
½ cup raisins
1 egg
1 cup milk
¼ cup sugar
dash nutmeg
¼ tsp salt

Bring the water to a boil. Add the salt, rice and raisins. Boil for 3 minutes, then let stand on the back of the stove until the rice is tender.

Beat the egg slightly and add to the rice. Add the sugar and milk and stir well.

Turn into a greased pudding pan, dot with butter, sprinkle with nutmeg and bake in a hot oven for 30 minutes.

Thick Milk Buns

2 cups flour
¾ cup thick milk (or enough to make a stiff dough)
1½ tsp baking soda
1 tsp salt
¼ cup butter, rendered pork fat or lard

Put the flour in a bowl. Rub in the butter or other fats of your choice. Add the salt. Add the soda to the thick milk and stir until it foams. Pour into the flour mixture and tumble until the flour is dampened evenly.

Grease a flat baking pan or large iron frying pan.

Turn the dough out on a floured board and press out with the hands to fit the pan. Cut into squares with a sharp knife. Prick each square with the tines of a fork.

Bake in a moderately hot oven. Turn out on a clean cloth and break into squares while hot.

If the thick milk is not sour, add ½ teaspoon of vinegar before mixing with the soda.

Serve hot with fresh butter or break the buns in two and spread with jam.

Pork Cakes

Pork cakes and a couple of watered scrawds made a hearty lunch for a fisherman's bread-box.

4 cups flour
4 tsps baking powder
½ lb salt pork
cold water

Cut the pork in small cubes and rinse it in warm water to remove the excess salt.

Render out the pork cubes on an iron frying pan. To render, place the pork cubes on an iron pan and put in the oven at moderate heat. The cubes should not be fried brown but rather white and soft.

Put flour and baking powder into a bowl. Mix lightly. Cool the pork cubes and fat and mix thoroughly through the flour. Add enough cold water to make a stiff dough.

Break off pieces of dough (equal in size) and form into balls. Place on a greased pan and bake in a hot oven.

Brown Bread

1 cup oatmeal
4 level tbsp fat
1 cup boiling water
4 tsps salt
5 tbsps brown sugar
¾ cup molasses
1½ cups warm water
1 yeast cake dissolved in ½ cup warm water and 1 tsp sugar
6 cups flour

Put the oatmeal and fat in a bowl, pour in the boiling water and stir. Add the salt, brown sugar, molasses and warm water.

When the mixture has cooled to lukewarm, add the dissolved yeast cake.

Lastly, add the flour and mix well. Form into loaves and put in greased pans. Cover and let rise.

Bake in a moderate oven until the crust is slightly brown.

Currant Tops

3 cups flour
¼ cup sugar
3 tsps baking powder
½ tsp salt
½ cup butter
1 cup milk
1 egg
1 cup currants

Soak the currants in 1 cup of cold water and drain when they are inflated slightly.

Sift the flour, sugar, baking powder and salt into a bowl. Mix in the butter with the fingertips. Add the currants. Beat the egg and add to the milk. Stir the liquid into the flour mixture and mix well.

Put on a floured board and pat to ¾ inch thickness. Cut in rounds and place on a flat bake pan. Brush with milk and bake in a hot oven for 15 minutes.

Sweet Bread

12 cups flour
1 cup molasses
3 cups water
¼ cup sugar
4 tsps salt
¼ cup butter or lard
1 cake yeast
1 cup lukewarm water
2 tsps sugar

Dissolve the yeast in 1 cup of lukewarm water to which 2 teaspoons of sugar has been added. Add enough flour to make a soft butter. Let rise. Add the molasses to 3 cups of water and heat until warm. Add the butter. Mix the salt, sugar and flour together in a bread pan. Add the yeast mixture. Pour one half of the liquid into the flour and yeast mixture and stir slightly. Add the remainder of the liquid, mix thoroughly with the hands and knead until the dough is smooth. Cover and let rise in a warm place overnight.

Punch down the dough next morning and turn out on a floured board. Knead and form into loaves. Put in greased loaf pans and let rise to the edge of the pans.

Bake in a medium hot oven until crusty and brown. Remove from the oven and brush with butter while hot.

Rhubarb Pie

2 cups flour
1 cup lard
2 cups chopped rhubarb
¾ cup sugar
dash cloves or nutmeg
cold water

*For best results, the lard should be as cold as possible. In St.
Leonard's, the lard was chilled by suspending the required amount
in a container, above the water-line of a water barrel or put in the
well-house overnight.*

Mix the flour and lard together in a bowl, rubbing the lard through the
flour until the mixture resembles coarse crumbs. Add enough cold water
to make a firm dough.

Work fast and handle the dough as little as possible. Divide into two
equal portions.

Roll out on a lightly floured board until the dough is very thin. Do not
push while rolling. The weight of your hands and the motion should
produce a nice thin pastry if the dough is the right consistency.

To make the filling, remove the leaves from the rhubarb stalks. Wash
the stalks in cold water, then cut into 1 inch chunks and drain.

Allow 3 cups of rhubarb to 1 cup of sugar and mix together in a bowl.

Place the pastry on two greased pie pans, making sure the pastry is
slightly larger than the pan.

Spoon the rhubarb mixture on top of the pastry and sprinkle with
cinnamon or nutmeg.

Roll out the remaining dough and cut it to fit over the filling.

Tuck in the edge of the bottom pastry and flute with the thumb and
forefinger. Pierce the centre with a sharp knife to allow steam to escape.

Bake the pie in a hot oven until the pastry is crisp and brown.

Boiled Cocoa Cake

 1 cup raisins
 1 cup currants
 ½ cup citron
 2 cups sugar
 2 tsps cloves
 ¼ cup cocoa
 1 tsp cinnamon
 1 tsp allspice
 ½ tsp nutmeg
 1 cup butter
 ½ cup lard

Mix these ingredients and simmer for 20 minutes. Then let them cool.

Add 2 teaspoons of baking soda to 4 cups of flour and sift well. Add the flour to the fruit mixture bit by bit with 1½ cups of warm water.

Put the mixture in an iron bake pot lined with greased brown paper and bake in a slow oven for 3 hours.

Boiled Molasses Cake

 4 cups flour
 2 cups molasses
 1 cup butter
 1 cup sour milk
 1 cup raisins
 1 cup currants
 ½ cup citron
 2 eggs
 2 tsps allspice
 2 tsps mixed spice
 2 tsps soda

Put the molasses, fruit, butter and spices in a saucepan. Heat to the boiling point and allow to cool.

Sift the soda with the flour and add to the fruit mixture. Then add the beaten eggs and milk.

Bake for 2 hours in a covered iron pot in a medium hot oven.

Pie Pastry

2½ cups flour
¼ tsp salt
½ tbsp sugar
1 cup lard or beef drippings
1 egg (beaten)

Sift the dry ingredients into a bowl. Cut in the shortening. Put the egg into a 1 cup measure. Add the water to make ½ cup of liquid. Beat lightly with a fork. Add the water and egg mixture to the flour and toss lightly until all the flour is dampened. Knead lightly and roll out to desired thickness.

This recipe will be sufficient to make 2 double pie crusts.

Cornmeal Cake

Corn meal or yellow meal, as it was usually called, was used in various ways.

It was used as a breakfast meal in the same manner as oatmeal. Sometimes it was served as a mug-up before bedtime on cold winter nights. On such an occasion, it was boiled like porridge, then sprinkled with brown sugar or molasses.

It was also made into Johnny Cakes for the youngsters' school lunches.

1 cup flour
1 cup yellow meal
2 tsps baking powder
¼ cup brown sugar
½ cup molasses
¼ cup lard or butter
½ tsp salt
cold milk

Put the flour, yellow meal, baking powder, salt and sugar in a bowl. Rub in the lard or butter until the mixture is crumbly. Add the molasses and mix well.

Add enough milk to make a medium dough. Press into a square pan and bake in a moderate oven until the top is nicely browned.

Cut it into squares and help yourself.

Molasses Pie

*When the supply of preserved berries ran out, housewives came up with
a healthy and tasty substitute for pie filling which was made from:*

½ cup of grated bread crumbs
1 egg
1 cup molasses
dash grated nutmeg
dash cinnamon

Heat the molasses but do not let it boil. Cool it slightly and add the beaten
egg, bread crumbs and spices.

Line a pie plate with pastry. Pour the molasses mixture over the
unbaked pastry.

Cut left-over pastry in strips. Twist the strips and lay criss-cross over
the filling. Press the moistened edge of the pastry with a fork and bake the
pie in a hot oven until the crust turns brown around the edge.

Cottage Pudding

1 cup flour
¼ cup lard
¼ tsp salt
1 egg (beaten)
½ cup sugar
¼ cup milk or water
2 tsps baking powder

Mix the sugar and lard together. Add the egg and mix well. Sift the flour,
baking powder and salt together and add to the first mixture, stirring with a
spoon. Add the milk and mix it well into the flour mixture.

Bake in a greased loaf pan on medium heat. Serve with molasses coady
or jam.

Molasses Coady

Bring 1 cup of molasses to a boil. Remove from the heat and add a dab of butter.

Plain Country Buns

½ lb salt pork (cut in small cubes)
6 cups white flour
2 level tsps baking soda
1½ cups water

Sift the flour and baking soda into a bowl. Rinse the pork cubes in warm water. Strain and add to the flour. Stir the water into the flour mixture to make a firm dough. Add more water in small quantities if necessary.

Turn out on a floured board and knead lightly. Press the dough out with the palms of the hands and cut into rounds with a bun cutter or a small water glass dipped in flour.

Place closely together on a greased baking sheet and bake until browned.

Molasses Country Buns

½ lb salt pork (cut in small cubes)
6 cups white flour
2 tsps soda
1 cup molasses
½ cup hot water

Heat the molasses to lukewarm. Sift the flour and baking powder into a bowl. Rinse the pork cubes in warm water. Strain and add to the flour.

Make a hollow in the flour mixture and pour in the molasses. Add the soda to the hot water and pour in with the molasses. Mix together with the hands until the dough is firm. Press out on a floured board and cut into rounds or press the dough into a deep bun pan and cut into squares.

Bake in a moderate oven and break apart while still hot.

Buttermilk Buns

4 cups flour
1½ cups buttermilk
1 tsp salt
2 tsps baking powder (if the buttermilk is sweet)
1½ tsps baking soda (if the buttermilk is sour)

Buttermilk is rich in fat content. There is no need to add additional fats to produce a light and flaky bun.

Sift flour, salt and baking powder (or baking soda) together in a bowl. Add the buttermilk slowly and mix lightly with the fingertips. If the buttermilk is thick and contains small particles of butter, you may need more than 1½ cups to produce a medium soft dough.

Place the dough on a floured board. Spread a little butter on the palms of the hands and knead the dough gently. Press out to desired thickness and cut into rounds with a bun cutter.

Place ½ inch apart on a greased bun pan and bake in a hot oven until browned on all sides.

Blueberry Grunt

2 cups flour
¾ cup butter
1 tsp salt
3 tsps baking powder
½ cup sugar
1 egg
enough cold water to make a soft dough

Place the flour and butter in a bowl and work in the butter with the tips of the fingers until the mixture is like coarse crumbs. Add the salt, sugar and baking powder and mix lightly.

Add the egg to ¼ cup of cold water and whisk with a fork until the yolk is broken. Add to the dry ingredients together with enough cold water to make a soft dough.

Divide the dough into two equal portions. Turn out on a floured board. Press the dough with the heel of the hand to about ½ inch thickness. Place over the bottom and sides of a greased 12 x 9 x 2 inch pan. Cut dough to fit by slicing along the edge of the pan with a sharp knife.

To make the filling, mix 3 cups of blueberries with 1 cup of sugar. Place the mixture on the pastry in the pan, covering all areas. Take the remaining dough and roll out on a floured board. Lay it over the blueberry and sugar mixture. Trim the edges and flute with the thumb and forefinger. Prick the centre with a fork and bake in a hot oven until golden brown.

To prevent the bottom pastry from becoming soggy, sprinkle it with rice or barley before adding the blueberry mixture.

Light Fruit Cake

½ cup butter
4 cups flour
2 tsps baking soda
2 cups brown sugar
2 cups sour milk
1 tsp vanilla
2 tsps cinnamon
1 tsp cloves
1 tsp spice
1 lb raisins
1 lb currants
½ lb citron

Cream the butter and the sugar. Sift the flour, soda, cinnamon, cloves and spice together. Add to the creamed mixture alternately with the sour milk. Mix thoroughly and add the raisins, currants and citron. Mix the fruit evenly through the batter.

Grease a bake pot and line with 2 layers of greased brown paper. Pour in the cake batter and spread evenly with a moist spoon.
Bake in a slow oven until done. Let the cake cool in the pot, then turn out on a platter and remove the paper. Allow to age for a couple of weeks.

Icing

2 egg whites
1 cup sugar
1 tsp vanilla

Beat egg whites until stiff, add sugar and vanilla. Spread generously over the top and sides of the cake. Shake ¼ of a cup of "tens of thousands" on the top for decoration.

Steamed Partridge Berry Pudding

1½ cups flour
3 tsps baking powder
¼ tsp salt
¼ cup butter
1¼ cup partridge berries
¾ cup milk

Sift the flour, baking powder and salt into a bowl. Rub in the butter. Add the berries, then the milk and stir all together.

Pour into a greased pudding mould and steam for 1 hour. Serve with a dab of jam or plain Sugar Sauce.

Sugar Sauce

½ cup of white sugar
1 cup cold water
1 tsp vanilla flavouring

Put the sugar and cold water in a saucepan and boil until the mixture begins to thicken.

Add the flavouring, stir and serve.

Molasses Suet Pudding

½ cup suet (cut fine)
2 cups white flour
1 tsp baking soda
½ tsp baking powder
½ tsp allspice
½ tsp cinnamon
½ tsp salt
½ cup molasses
½ cup water
½ cup raisins or currants

Combine the flour and suet in a bowl. Add the soda, baking powder, salt and spices. Stir the water into the molasses and add to the flour mixture. Add the raisins and mix through the dough thoroughly

Turn a pudding bag inside out and dip in cold water. (This prevents the pudding from sticking to the bag in the process of cooking.)

Spoon the pudding mixture into the bag, gather loosely at the top and tie tightly with a string. Place a saucer or small plate in a pot of boiling water. Put the pudding on the saucer and boil for one hour.

If cooked properly, the pudding should be easily shaken from the bag. Serve with meat dinners or as a dessert with Sugar Sauce.

Boiled Bread Pudding

left-over bread
water
2 tbsps pork drippings (or suet)
1 tsp baking powder
½ tsp salt
¼ cup flour

Take some dried bread or left-over heels of bread and soak in cold water until soft. Strain off the water and press out as much moisture as possible.

Put the soaked bread in a bowl and add the pork drippings or suet. (2 cups of soaked bread will be sufficient) Add 1 tsp of baking powder and ½ teaspoon of salt to ¼ cup of flour.

Mix these ingredients into the soaked bread with a wooden spoon. Put the mixture into a pudding bag (dampened with water) and press firmly. Gather the bag tightly at the top and tie with a string.

Place in the pot with a salt beef dinner or cook separately in boiling water. The time for cooking by either method is about ¾ of an hour.

Plain Suet Pudding

1½ cups white flour
½ cup suet (cut fine)
2 tsps baking powder
1 tsp salt
½ cup water

Mix flour and suet together in a bowl. Add the baking powder and salt. Add the cold water and mix with a wooden spoon.

Put in a greased pudding steamer and cook for 1 hour.

Hert Tarts

Hert is simply another name for the blueberry. It may have been more commonly used in some Newfoundland places than in others.

2 cups flour
¾ cup lard or rendered salt pork fat
dash salt
cold water
1 to 1½ cups hert jam
muffin pan or 12 muffin cups

Place flour, lard and salt in a bowl. Mix with the fingertips until the contents become coarse and crumbly. Add enough cold water to make a stiff dough.

Roll the dough on a floured board until it is very thin. Cut in circles 1 inch larger than the muffin cups. Place each circle in a greased cup and press lightly to shape. Fill with a couple of tablespoons of hert jam. Cross each cup with strips of left-over pastry. Crimp the edges or press together with the tines of a fork.

Bake in a hot oven until crisp and brown.

The secret of good pastry is to have the lard or fat (as you prefer) and the water as cold as possible. Use the rolling pin lightly and with quick short strokes. If you haven't got a rolling pin, use an empty whisky bottle sprinkled lightly with flour.

This recipe was used for making pies with a variety of store bought fillings such as dried apples and dried apricots.

Doughballs

The amount of flour used to make doughballs was geared to the number of people to be served. They were served with fresh meat or salt meat dinners and also as a dessert with Molasses Coady or jam.

3 cups white flour
3½ tsps baking powder
1 tsp salt

Mix the ingredients together in a bowl and add enough cold water to form a firm dough.

Shape into balls and cook in the liquid of salt meat dinners if that is the meal you are serving. If you want to serve doughballs with fresh meat, place them on the meat before you thicken the gravy. If you want to try them as a dessert, drop them in boiling salted water.

The cooking time for all occasions is about 15 to 18 minutes.

Planter's Bread

2 cups dried hops
2 cups water
1 tsp sugar
flour
10 to 12 cups flour
2 tbsps coarse salt
¼ cup sugar
2 tbsps lard
2 cups lukewarm water

To make the barm, steep 2 cups of dried hops in 2 cups of water. Strain and let cool to lukewarm. Use only the liquid. Discard the lees. Add 1 teaspoon of sugar and enough flour to make a soft batter. Let rise in a warm place.

Put 10 to 12 cups of flour in a mixing pan. Add 2 tablespoons of ground coarse salt and ¼ cup of sugar. Cover and lay aside.

When the barm has risen, add 2 tablespoons of melted lard to 2 cups of lukewarm water and add to the flour. Do not stir at this point. Add the barm and mix all ingredients together.

Place the dough mixture on a floured board and knead well. Use a dusting of flour to keep the dough from sticking to the board. Put the dough back in the bread pan and let rise overnight. Wrap warmly and keep free from drafts.

Next morning, punch down the dough and prepare the baking pans. Seasoned bread pans should rarely be washed and should be dark in colour to produce an even brown crusty load. Warm the baking pans and grease with lard or rendered fat.

Turn the dough out on a floured board and knead for 10 minutes to remove air bubbles. Cut the dough into uniform pieces. Roll each piece with the hands, tucking in the edges to form a ball. Put them into the baking pans and let rise to the edge.

Bake in a moderately hot oven until done and place on a rack to cool.

This recipe was used when baking was done with wood stoves. A
housewife would gauge her own temperature and timing according
to her experience with her stove.

Tea Loaf

 2 cups strong tea
 1 cup raisins
 2½ cups white flour
 1 cup sugar
 2 tsps nutmeg
 2 tsps cinnamon
 ½ tsp cloves
 2 tsps soda
 1 tsp salt
 ½ cup lard or butter

Add the hot tea to the raisins and let cool. Mix flour, sugar, spices, soda and salt together in a bowl. Add the lard and rub into the flour mixture. Add the tea and raisins. Stir until all the flour has been dampened.

Put into a greased loaf pan and bake in a moderate oven for about 1 hour.

If you want to test the loaf, pierce with a steel knitting needle. If the needle comes out free of dough, the loaf is done.

Pancakes

   1 cup milk
   1 cup flour
   2 tbsp butter
   1 tsp baking powder
   1 egg
   1 tbsp white sugar
   pinch salt

Sift the flour, salt, sugar and baking powder together in a bowl. Mix in the butter, beat the egg and add to the flour mixture. Add the milk and stir well through the dry ingredients.

Drop ½ cup of the batter on a slightly greased frying pan. Turn when bubbles appear. Fry on both sides until lightly browned.

A cup of blueberries added to the batter before cooking made the pancakes something special.

Pancakes are served with a variety of jams and sauces. A dab of butter and hot molasses sauce was a favourite at home.

Bakeapple Jam

*Bakeapples ripened early in August. The area in which they grew
was referred to as the "bakeapple mash." It took quite a while to
pick a gallon after the berry had turned yellow and soft. So, many
trips were made to the "mash" to make sure they were picked before
they ripened to that stage.*

*The priest or the magistrate might pay .50 cents a gallon for
bakeapples and maybe the local merchant would let the children
"take up" the worth of the amount picked in something of their
choice from the store.*

*Jam was made when the berries were in the soft, yellow stage.
A ½ cup of sugar to 1 cup of bakeapples produced a tart succulent
preserve. It made a very special dessert when served with scalded
cream.*

Blackberry Pudding

Blackberry was the local name for the heath berry. They grew on dry turf areas and hung shining black and tempting on toe-hold edges of the cliff-face. The inky juice dyed your tongue, lips and fingers and as they were the first berry to ripen they were a favourite of the children in the Cove.

> **2 cups flour**
> **2½ tsps baking powder**
> **½ cup sugar**
> **¼ tsp salt**
> **1 egg**
> **½ cup water**
> **1 cup blackberries**
> **1 tbsp butter**

Sift the flour, baking powder, salt and sugar into a bowl. Mix in the butter and beaten egg with a wooden spoon. Add the water and mix well. Add the blackberries and distribute through the dough.

Put into a damp pudding bag and boil for 1 hour.

Serve with a salt beef dinner or as a dessert with Sugar Sauce or a sprinkling of brown sugar.

Tea Buns

1 egg
2 cups flour
¾ cup butter
½ cup sugar
4 tsps baking powder
1 tsp salt
cold water

Place flour and butter in a bowl. Mix thoroughly with the fingertips until the mixture is crumbly. Add the sugar and salt and mix lightly. Add the baking powder and whisk through the flour mixture.

Break 1 egg (unbeaten) and drop it in. Add cold water, a little at a time and mix to form a soft dough.

Place dough on a floured board and press out with the palms of the hands to about ¾ inch thickness. Cut into rounds with floured cutter or small glass. Place close together on a greased bun pan and bake in a hot oven for 15 minutes.

The secret of delicate and tasty tea buns depends on the least amount of kneading and the use of very cold water for mixing.

Cinnamon Rolls

Make dough as in the recipe for tea buns.

Roll out on a floured board until the dough is about ¼ inch thick. Spread all over with soft butter. Sprinkle ½ cup of brown sugar over the butter and shake 1 tablespoon of cinnamon all over.

Roll up, beginning at the narrow end, using a little pressure. Cut into circles and place flat side down on a baking sheet.

Bake in a hot oven for 15 minutes. Let cool in the pan, then store in a crock or glass jar.

Raisin Bread

1 lb raisins
10 cups flour
3 cups water
1 cup milk
4 tsps salt
½ cup sugar
¼ lb butter
1 yeast cake
½ cup lukewarm water
1 tsp sugar

Put the flour in a large pan. Make sure it is at room temperature. Add the salt. Rub in the butter and add the sugar. Add the raisins and mix all together with a wooden spoon. Heat 3 cups of water and 1 cup of milk together until warm.

Add the yeast to ½ cup of lukewarm water. Add 1 teaspoon of sugar and set aside to dissolve. Add enough flour to make a batter and let rise for half an hour.

Make a hollow in the flour, pour in the yeast mixture and ½ the amount of warm water. Mix through the flour with a spoon. Add the remaining water and mix with the hands until all the flour is dampened. Knead to a firm dough. Form into a ball. Spread a little butter over the top, cover and set to rise in a warm place. If bread is made in the morning, let it rise for 5 hours.

When the dough has risen to the top of the pan, punch it down and prepare the baking pans. Turn the dough out on a floured board and knead lightly. Form into loaves and put into warm greased pans to rise.

Let rise for ½ an hour, then bake in a moderately hot oven until the loaves have an even brown crust.

Turn out on a clean cloth and brush with melted butter.

Grandma's Gingerbread

½ cup pork fat
1½ cups molasses
1 egg (beaten)
3 cups flour
½ tsp salt
1½ tsps baking powder
½ tsp baking soda
1 tsp cinnamon
1 tsp ginger
½ tsp cloves
½ cup hot water

Rub the fat into the flour. Add the baking powder and salt and mix lightly. Add the beaten egg to the molasses, then add the spices and mix. Add this mixture to the flour and blend well. Lastly, add the soda mixed with the hot water and stir.

Bake in an 8 by 10 by 2 inch pan in a moderate oven until done. Let cool in the pan and cut in squares.

Caraway Bread

Caraway blossoms were picked and hung in paper bags to dry. The seed of the blossoms dropped to the bottom of the bag and were sifted and stored in jars for using as a flavour in bread, buns and biscuits.

1 yeast cake
1 cup lukewarm water
2 tsps sugar
flour (enough to make a batter)

10 cups flour
2 cups water
2 cups molasses
3 tsps salt
¼ cup lard or butter
¼ cup caraway seeds

Dissolve the yeast in lukewarm water. Add the sugar and stir. Add enough flour to make a batter and set aside for ½ hour. Put the flour in a large bowl or bread pan. Add the salt and caraway seeds. Rub the lard or butter into the flour. Heat the water and molasses together until warm.

Add the yeast mixture to the flour and pour in ½ the water and molasses mixture. Mix lightly with a wooden spoon. Add the remaining liquid and mix with the hands until the dough is smooth and easy to handle. Grease the top with a little butter, cover well and let rise overnight.

Next morning, punch down the dough and prepare the baking pans. Turn the dough out on a floured board and knead for 10 minutes. Form into loaves and put them in the pans. Let rise to the top edge of the pans and bake in a moderate oven.

Blueberry Buckle

1 cup flour
1½ tsps baking powder
pinch salt
1/3 cup milk
¼ cup butter
1 egg
1/3 cup sugar

Filling:

2 cups blueberries
1 cup sugar
½ tsp cinnamon

Topping:

½ cup of sugar
¼ cup butter
4 tbsp flour

Mix the butter and sugar until soft. Add the egg and beat well with an egg beater. Add the salt and baking powder to the flour and sift together. Add to the butter and egg mixture. Add the milk and blend well. Put this batter in a square pan.

Mix the blueberries and sugar together and spread over the batter. Sprinkle with cinnamon.

Mix the ingredients for the topping together until crumbly and sprinkle over the filling. Bake in a moderate oven until the topping is slightly brown (about 30 minutes).

Partridge berries, marsh berries or raspberries may be used for this recipe, but if you use either one of these for the filling, omit the cinnamon.

St. Leonard's Revisited

We came ashore
where wildflower hills
tilted to the tide
and walked
sad and gay
among the turnip cellars
tripping over the cremated
foundations
of long-ago homes
half buried
in the long years' grass

Almost reverently
we walked among the rocks
of the holy church
and worshipped roses
in the dead yard
and came again to the cove
as they did after rosary
in the green and salty days

And men offshore
hauling traps
wondered what ghosts
we were
walking with the forgotten sheep
over the thigh-high grass paths
that led
like trap doors
to a past
they could hardly recall

Written by Al Pittman on the occasion of his first visit home to St. Leonard's after the people had left. Reprinted with the author's permission.

Glossary

ballycarter — (ballycater) ice on or along the shore.

boogie — a potbellied stove.

bracken — common fern.

brouse — young trees (fir and birch) on which rabbits, goats and sheep commonly feed.

caplin scull — the annual spawning of the caplin (a small silver bellied fish). In early summer millions of these fish spawn upon and near the beaches of Newfoundland. They are harvested by hand, dipnets and cast nets for use as food, bait and fertilizer.

collar — a length of rope some yards off-shore to which boats were moored.

connors — species of fish inhabiting inshore waters especially around wharves and stages.

copper — (my punt) to paint the punt (boat) with anti-fouling ' copper ' paint.

corking — (the boat) common usage of the word caulking, i.e. to make a boat leakproof by caulking the seams with oakum.

devils darn' needles — (or darning needles) a bluish flying insect much like a dragon fly but smaller.

droke — a stand of timber where wood for a variety of purposes could be procured.

googs — small white egg-shaped berries; the fruit of the maiden-hair fern. It has an unusual minty, wintergreen flavour.

hare bells — small blue, bell-like wildflower found growing in niches along the cliffs.

hoars eggs — (or whore's eggs) sea urchins.

longer — long wooden poles used as fence railings and in the construction of stages and flakes.

marsh rush — the rushes (reeds) that grow on the marshes.

May flower — white and pink wildflowers. One of the earliest wildflowers to bloom in spring, often used to decorate altars dedicated to the Blessed Virgin.

oakum — a hemp like fibrous material used for caulking seams in the hull of a boat.

pit props — timber used for propping up the ceiling of mining pits (shafts).

puncheon — large cask

scale — (of tobacco) the outer leaf wrapping of a plug of tobacco.

shift — (for men) a complete change of clothes.

slacked lime — a solution of lime and water.

splits — kindling, wood split with an axe to a size useful for starting a fire.

strouter — upright timber foundation of wharves, stages, etc.

tan pots — large iron pots in which bark was boiled to make a tanning solution; nets were immersed in the solution to preserve them.

tolepins — tholepins, wooden pegs used as oarlocks in any kind of row boat.

Virgin flower — a cream coloured small wildflower often found growing in mossy areas.